2

The Language Kit

Writing through Grammar

John Seely

Heinemann

Heinemann Educational Publishers
Halley Court, Jordan Hill, Oxford OX2 8EJ
A division of Reed Educational and Professional Publishing Ltd

OXFORD MELBOURNE AUCKLAND
JOHANNESBURG BLANTYRE GABORONE
IBADAN PORTSMOUTH NH (USA) CHICAGO

03 02 01 00 99
10 9 8 7 6 5 4 3 2

ISBN 0 435 10199 4

Designed and produced by Ken Vail Graphic Design
Cover design by I E Design
Cover illustration by Anthony Rule
Illustrated by Graham-Cameron Illustration (Michelle Ives and Brian Lee), Deborah Hinks, Elizabeth Roy Literary Agency (Mike Phillips) and Anthony Rule.
Original illustrations © Heinemann Educational Publishers 1999
Printed and bound in Spain by Edelvives

Tel:01865 888058 email:info.he@heinemann.co.uk

Acknowledgements

With special thanks to Royal Manor School, Portland, Tendring Technology College, Landermere, and Monks' Dyke Technology College, Louth, for commenting on and trialing material.

The authors and publishers would like to thank the following for permission to reproduce copyright material:
Aladdin Books Limited for an extract from *Hurricanes and Tidal Waves* by J Dineen; Blanford Press Limited for the chapter 'Mexico' from *Christmas*; Chichester Harbour Conservancy for extracts from a publicity guide; Dorling Kindersley Limited for extracts from *Eye Witness – Future* by Michael Tambini. Text © Michael Tambini 1998; The Economist Publications Limited and Webster's Traveller's Guides Limited for an extract from *The Economic Guide: Britain*, 2nd Edition; Element Children's Books for extracts from *Dead Giveaways* by Andrew Donkin, 1998; Evans Brothers Limited, London, for extracts from *The World of Festivals – Divali* by Dilip Kadodwala, 1998; Guardian Media Group for an extract from *Observer Life*, 8.11.98; Heinemann Educational for an extract from *Celebrate Christian Festivals* by Jan Thompson, and extracts from *The Stuarts (History Series)* by Andrew Langley; Hodder and Stoughton Limited for extracts from *Activators: Ballet* by Victoria Parker; from *Activators: Riding* by Sarah Gaydon; from *Activators: Skateboarding* by James Marsh; from *What's the Big Idea: Genetics* by Martin Brookes; and from *What's the Big Idea: Virtual Reality* by Chris Oxlade; IPC International Syndication for extracts from *Now Magazine* 'The World's Most Beautiful People' 1998, © Now Magazine/IPC Magazines Ltd; Kingfisher Publications for adapted illustrations and text from 'Solitaire' in *The Superbook of Games to Make and Play* by Pia Hsiao, Neil Lorimer and Nick Williams 1987; Macmillan General Books for extracts from *Coasting* by Jonathan Raban (Picador, 1995); Mainstream Publishing Company (Edinburgh) Limited for extracts from *Dear Country* by Harry Reid; Observer Newspapers for a news item in the *Chichester Observer*, 22.10.87; Penguin Books Limited for an adapted extract from *The Young Green Consumer Guide* by John Elkington, Julia Hailes with Douglas Hill (Victor Gollancz/Hamish Hamilton). Copyright © John Elkington, Julia Hailes, Douglas Hill 1990; Portsmouth City Council for extracts from the *Portsmouth*; Reader's Digest Limited for an extract from *Treasures of Britain*; The Rough Guides for an extract from *Rough Guide to Britain*, 2nd Edition, 1998; Scholastic Children's Books for extracts from *Horrible Science: Fatal Forces* by Nick Arnold, illustrations by Tony de Saulles. Text © Nick Arnold 1997 and Illustrations © Tony de Saulles 1997; extract from *Ugly Bugs* by Nick Arnold. Text © Nick Arnold, 1996, Illustrations © Tony de Saulles 1996, first published by Scholastic Ltd. Words are missing in the extract that appear in the original; for extracts from *Horrible Histories: The Slimy Stuarts* by Terry Deary. Text © Terry Deary 1996; and for extracts from *Smashin' Fashion* by Michael Cox. Text © Michael Cox 1998; Trans-edition Limited and Fernleigh Books for an extract from *Religions of the World* by Breuilly, O'Brien and Palmer; Transworld Publishers Limited for extracts from *Notes from a Small Island* by Bill Bryson. Copyright © Bill Bryson 1995. (Black Swan, a division of Transworld Limited). All rights reserved; Walker Books Limited for extracts from *Smokestack Lightening* by Lawrence Staig. Copyright © 1992 by Lawrence Staig; for extracts from *Pig Ignorant* by Nicholas Fisk. Copyright © 1992 by Nicholas Fisk; and for extracts from *Ordinary Sea Man* by John Gordon. Copyright © 1992 by John Gordon.

The publishers have made every effort to trace the copyright holders, but if they have inadvertently overlooked any, they will be pleased to make the necessary arrangements at the first opportunity.

The publishers would also like to thank the following for permission to reproduce photographs on the pages noted:

John Seely, p16-17; Andes Press Agency/Irit Sapir, p56; Sally & Richard Greenhill, p56; CIRCA Photo Library/John Smith, p56; Roger Scruton, p57, 97, 152; Nial McInerney, p112.

Contents

UNIT 9 — 87

UNIT 10 — 97

UNIT 11 — 105

UNIT 12 — 115

UNIT 13 — 125

UNIT 14 — 135

UNIT 15 — 145

Grammar reference

A message for teachers

The Language Kit contains teaching materials that help you to teach grammatical concepts and to guide pupils in using this understanding of grammar in their reading and writing. Since grammar is a system it has to be introduced systematically. This means that the book is progressive; each unit assumes that the material in earlier units has been fully understood.

There are fifteen units, of which twelve are teaching units and three – numbers 5, 10 and 15 – are revision units. Each unit has ten pages.

The teaching units are based on the adventures of an Eastern European TV director called Yuri. He has come to Britain to make a series of programmes for HERZEGOVINATV. Unfortunately his knowledge of English is limited and so he needs a lot of help with the language. This device is used to enable pupils to reflect upon and articulate their existing knowledge of English.

Each of the teaching units follows a similar pattern:

A: Introductory page

The first page contains a large picture illustrating some aspect of Yuri's exploration of life in Britain, followed by a small number of discussion points to get the class talking about the chosen situation. There is also a summary of the language content of the unit.

B: Language awareness

The first spread focuses on some aspect of language usage and invites pupils to reflect upon and discuss it in a structured way.

C: Grammar study

The next spread introduces and teaches the grammatical material of the unit.

D: Grammar and sentences

This spread gives pupils a chance to practise the grammar they have just learned, by completing sentences and/or writing their own.

E: Drafting and writing

The final spread contains a structured approach to writing in a particular mode or format. This is usually linked to both the language awareness and grammatical content of the unit.

F: Final page

This contains a summary of the main language points covered.

On each spread the material is progressively more demanding. Usually on the language awareness, grammar study and grammar and sentences pages, the essential material is covered on the left-hand page, while the right-hand page contains important extension material. So all pupils can work on the left-hand page material and the more able can cover both pages. The Teacher's Book indicates when this pattern is not followed.

The revision units can be used as informal tests for individual work, or for reinforcement work with the class as a whole. There are additional tests in the Teacher's Book. These can be photocopied as required.

If you have any comments on these materials and suggestions for their improvement, I should be most grateful to hear from you, via the publisher.

Meet Yuri

Yuri

Yuri comes from Eastern Europe. He is a very successful TV director from HERZEGOVINATV. He has come to this country to make a series of programmes about our language and our way of life. He plans to make one 30-minute programme a fortnight. He is going to be helped by two British assistants:

- Gofer is the one who does all the running around and operates the camera.
- Sarah-Jane is the cool, organized one, who makes sure everything runs smoothly.

In the picture you see Gofer and Sarah-Jane meeting Yuri at the airport. Gofer is pushing Yuri's trolley.

The book

In each unit of the book you will be asked to help Yuri in two different ways:

- by telling him about our way of life
- by explaining things about the English language.

Yuri thinks he speaks English very well, but, as you will see, his English is sometimes a bit odd.

1 UNIT 1

August: Yuri at the seaside

At the time Yuri arrived in this country, most people were off on their holidays. Yuri and the team decided to find out where people take their holidays and what they do.

- How would you explain the word 'holiday' to Yuri?
- Why do people have holidays?
- What kind of place do most people go to for their holidays?
- What do you like doing when you go on holiday?
- What is your idea of a 'dream holiday'?

In this unit you will learn about:

The language of the seaside

Looking at texts:

- where they come from
- who they are written for
- why they are written.

The complement of a sentence

Linking verbs

Building sentences from short phrases

Beside the seaside

Yuri has decided to make a short programme about seaside holidays. But he doesn't understand a lot of what he sees and hears. Perhaps you can help him.

Exercise A

Write a clear explanation of what each of these signs means. Remember that Yuri comes from a country where they don't have any of these things – it hasn't even got a coast!

1. Pier
2. Krazy Golf
3. Helter Skelter
4. Formula Fun Go-Karting
5. Underwater World
6. Windsurfing Centre
7. Pedalos for Hire
8. Bingo
9. Ghost Train
10. BurgerBar

Exercise B

Yuri wants to do some interviews with people who work at the seaside. But there are problems. Read the interview and then answer the questions.

YURI: Tell me, please what you do.
DAVE: I run this amusement arcade, don't I.
YURI: Yes, you do. What is amusement arcade?
DAVE: Well you've got all these slot machines …
YURI: Which slot machines … ?
DAVE: You know – games. You put a coin in the slot and you play a game.
YURI: Is what games?
DAVE: There's all sorts, aren't there. You've got your fruit machines –
YURI: My fruit machines?
DAVE: Yeah.
YURI: Fruit machine is machine full of fruit?

1. Yuri isn't very good at asking questions. Choose one of his questions and explain what it should be in correct English.
2. Dave is speaking in a slangy way. He uses expressions that Yuri misunderstands. Find one and explain how Yuri has misunderstood what Dave is saying.
3. Can you explain to Yuri what a fruit machine is? Write four or five sentences giving a clear explanation.

Reading about the seaside

Sarah-Jane has collected some things for Yuri to read. He finds them rather difficult and needs help.

Exercise A

Read each of the extracts and answer these questions about each one:

1. **Where** do you think it comes from?
2. **Who** is it written for?
3. **Why** is it written; what is its purpose? Is it:
   - to give information
   - to tell people what to do
   - to persuade people to think about things in a particular way
   - to provide entertainment
   - a mixture of these
   - or for some other purpose? (And, if so, what?)

1

Twice every 24 hours, the sea moves up the shore and then back again. These movements are called tides. They are controlled by the pull of the sun and moon on the earth. Every two weeks very strong 'spring' tides occur. (They have nothing to do with the season.) Neap tides occur between spring tides. Their rise and fall is shorter than spring tides.

2

FOLLOW THE COUNTRY CODE

- Guard against all risk of fire.
- Fasten all gates.
- Keep dogs under proper control.
- Keep to the paths across farm land.
- Avoid damaging fences, hedges and walls.
- Leave no litter …

3

Southsea's four mile promenade with its sweeping views across to the Solent and Isle of Wight attracts visitors all year round.

There is a mix of lively attractions. Clarence and South Parade Pier offer the best in traditional and modern seaside fun. The Pyramids complex is the place for a 'splashing' good time whatever the weather and offers an entertainment programme throughout the year. At the Sea Life Centre the whole family can get a little closer to the maritime world but watch out for those sharks!

4

ABBEYTON–FRAME FERRY TIMETABLE

The Ferry runs at weekends from 1st April to 30th September, starting at 10.00 and finishing at 18.00. From the second weekend in July to the second weekend in September the Ferry runs every day including weekends.

TIMETABLE FOR COLLECTIONS FROM ABBEYTON–FRAME HARD*

10.00	16.00
12.00	18.00
14.00	

*A 'hard' is a firm section of beach or river bank. Boats are pulled up onto it out of the water.

The sentence fruit machine

Sarah-Jane has given Yuri a new toy to help him with his English! It's a fruit machine with words instead of pictures. With this machine you win every time: however it stops, it makes a correct English sentence.

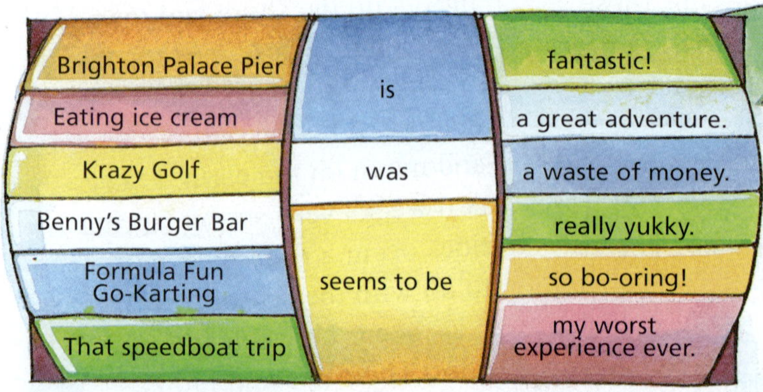

Exercise A

1. Try the machine: make a sentence using something from the first wheel, something from the second and something from the third.
2. Do it again and make two more sentences.

Exercise B

So far in *The Language Kit* we have looked at these sentence parts: subject, verb, object. What sentence part does the first wheel contain? And the second wheel?

The complement

You could have used the fruit machine to make this sentence:
Krazy Golf is a waste of money.

It has a subject: ***Krazy Golf***
a verb: ***is***
and something else: ***a waste of money***

The words 'a waste of money' tell us more about the subject. In fact, they complete it. So they are called the **complement** of the sentence.

Subject	Verb	Complement
That book	was	brilliant.
Your aunt	seems	very generous.
Mr Green	is	our English teacher.

Important: in sentences like this the subject and the complement are always about the same person, thing or idea.

More about the complement

The complement comes after the verb. It tells us more about the subject. One way of checking whether this is right is to do this:

1. Find the verb.
2. Cross it out and replace it with an equals sign.
3. If the sentence still has the same meaning, then the part after the verb (or equals sign) is the complement.

So:

That TV programme ~~was~~ = the best last year.

But if it doesn't work, you know you've gone wrong:

My grandfather ~~keeps~~ = a pig.

Linking verbs

The verb in a sentence that contains a complement is a **linking verb**. The commonest linking verb is 'to be':

am/is/are
was/were
has been/have been
etc.

Other verbs that can be used are:

become
appear
seem

Exercise C

Each of these sentences contains a subject, a verb and a complement. Write the sentences out in a table, like the one at the bottom of the previous page.

1. Talking during maths lessons is strictly against the rules.
2. Marie Peters is my best friend.
3. My cousin seems very happy.
4. Our back garden has become very overgrown.
5. That story is absolutely terrifying.

Exercise D

Part of each of these sentences is printed in **bold**. For each sentence write whether this part is the complement or the object of the sentence.

1. My cat's name is **Clarence.**
2. Clarence is **very aggressive.**
3. Yesterday he bit **the postman.**
4. The postman was **very upset.**
5. He told **the RSPCP.**
6. The RSPCP is **the Royal Society for the Prevention of Cruelty to Postmen.**

More complements

Exercise A

Yuri wants to make a children's programme about a seaside town. Sarah-Jane has collected some information for him. Unfortunately her computer has jumbled it up: each sentence now has the wrong complement. See if you can give each sentence the right complement so that the sentences make sense. Write the sentences out with the correct complement.

1. Portsea is at one end of the promenade.
2. It used to be a harbour for fishing boats.
3. Then the town became a little train to carry people from one end to the other.
4. At Portsea there is a popular seaside town.
5. It is about a mile long.
6. The promenade is a fishing village.
7. There is popular with tourists.

Exercise B

Now the computer has really gone mad! It has cut out a different section in each sentence. Work out what each sentence could be, and write the sentences out.

8. In the harbour there many different kinds of boat.
9. are fishing boats.
10. are leisure boats.
11. several different kinds of leisure boat.
12. The ones with two hulls are.
13. In the summer the sea should be.
14. In winter it may be.

Building sentences

Exercise A

Sarah-Jane has made some rough notes about a large seaside town. Now she wants to turn them into a short script, describing some of its attractions. The script will be heard as the TV screen shows pictures of the attractions – as 'voice-over'. Read the notes and then follow the instructions at the bottom of the page.

The notes

The Pier	
longest on the South Coast built over 120 years ago	theatre and nightclub two family entertainment centres
The castle	
built after the Norman Conquest beautiful lake and grounds with picnic site	Battle of Hastings Museum restaurant and shop
Prince Edward Harbour	
a working harbour for fishing boats trips along the coast 'Neptune's Kingdom' theme park	sailing and windsurfing lessons boats for hire
The Havisham Centre	
exciting leisure complex three pools and two flumes keep-fit centre and gymnasium	special holiday activities under-5s and under-10s clubs

What to do

Sarah-Jane has already started writing her script. It begins like this:

> Eastport is a traditional holiday centre on the South Coast offering a wide range of attractions. Whether you are young or old, active or lazy, Eastport has lots to offer. Every seaside resort has to have a pier and Eastport has one of the best. Built over a hundred and twenty years ago, the pier is the longest on the South Coast ...

1. Finish off the script about the pier.
2. Choose two of the other three attractions and write the script for them.

The harbour

Yuri is making a programme about harbours. He hopes it will be shown on British TV and he wants a short article to go into a TV listings magazine. (This is the kind of magazine that tells you what programmes are on and what they are about.) Yuri has asked you to write a short article about a harbour for this magazine. You can write about:

- a harbour you know
- one of the harbours in the pictures here and on the next page
- a harbour you have made up.

What to do

1. Decide on your subject.
2. Make a list of three or four main features.
3. For each feature make a list of details you could include.
4. Make a plan: write a few words for each feature, describing it.
5. Now write your first draft, describing each of your chosen features. On the opposite page there is a resource bank of words to help you.
6. When you have finished the first draft, read through what you have written. Check carefully that your description flows through from the beginning to the end and covers each feature properly. Rewrite where necessary.
7. Check for mistakes of spelling, punctuation and grammar.
8. Now write out a clean copy of your final version.

Resource bank

harbour
port
dock
wharf
lock
pier
quay
jetty
lighthouse
boathouse
warehouse
shed
shack
outbuilding
crane
souvenir shop
chandler's
café
pub
fish shop

concrete
stone
granite
iron
steel
brick
cobbles
slate
sand
mud
slime
ooze
shingle
pebble
silt

dinghy
fishing boat
trawler
tug
catamaran
ketch
sloop
yawl
sailboard
pram
smack
skiff
ferry
barge
trawler
lifeboat

rope
cable
chain
hawser
line
cord
painter
moorings

sunny
stormy
grey
bright
rain
drizzle
hail
snow
breeze
gale
squally
calm
choppy
white horses
waves
spume
spray

Summing up what you've learned

The sentence complement

The **complement** comes after the verb. It tells us more about the subject. One way of checking whether this is right is to do this:

1. Find the verb.
2. Cross it out and replace it with an equals sign.
3. If the sentence still has the same meaning, then the part after the verb (or equals sign) is the complement.

So:

That TV programme ~~was~~ = the best last year.

Linking verbs

If a sentence begins with a subject and ends with a complement, the verb that comes between them is called a **linking verb**. The commonest linking verb is 'to be':

am/is/are
was/were
has been/have been
will be, can be
etc.

Other verbs that can be used are:

become
appear
seem

Drafting guidelines

1. **Define your subject:**
   Make a list of three or four main features.
2. **Collect ideas:**
   For each feature make a list of details you could include.
3. **Make a plan:**
   - Decide on the order of features.
   - Sort the details you have listed for each feature.
   - Add fresh ideas.
4. **Write your first draft:**
   For each of your chosen features write three to five sentences.
5. **Check for content:**
   Read through what you have written. Make sure that it:
   - says what you want to say
   - hasn't missed out anything important
   - is in the right order.
6. **Rewrite where necessary.**
7. **Check for accuracy:**
   Look for mistakes of spelling, punctuation and grammar.
8. **Make a fair copy:**
   Write out a clean copy of your final version and pay attention to handwriting, headings and layout.

UNIT 2

Celebrity interview

So Yuri and the team are going to make a programme based on the life and work of a celebrity.

- What is a celebrity?
- Who would you say were celebrities?
- If you were Yuri, which celebrity would you choose to interview and why?

In this unit you will learn about:

Prepositions:

- what they are
- how we use them
- what they mean.

Paragraphs:

- why we use them when we write
- how to plan them
- how to write them.

Celebrity profiles

Sarah-Jane has been collecting some cuttings for Yuri to read. They're all about different kinds of celebrity.

Vanessa-Mae

She's so stylish and self-composed, Vanessa Mae could be any age from 18 to 35. But she's still only 19, although she already has a fearsome list of achievements on her CV: the youngest ever pupil at the Central Conservatoire of Music in Beijing (she was eight) and the most successful ever classical musician in the popular charts.

She's been based in London since her Thai father and Chinese mother split up when she was four, and admits that her new look is designed to please her mum. 'She finds my haircut very adorable and very cute.'

Adam Hollioake

Cricketer Adam Hollioake has been described as a cross between Keanu Reeves and George Clooney. With a taut, powerful body, the England one-day captain is obviously physically tough (he once left the pitch with blood streaming down his face, commenting simply: 'My head got in the way'). But Hollioake, 26, is mentally tough too, and desperate to win, whatever the contest. 'I despise losing,' he says.

Exercise A

This kind of writing uses a lot of **adjectives***. They are used to show the 'star qualities' of the person and to tell us how much the writer likes or admires the person described. For example:

She's so stylish and self-composed, Vanessa Mae could be any age from 18 to 35.

1. Look through the texts and find five adjectives showing how the writer approves of the person. Make sure to choose adjectives from all four texts.
2. Write the five adjectives down.

Exercise B

This kind of writing uses a lot of **nouns and noun phrases*** that tell us how much the writer likes or admires the person described. For example:

Bussell is known for her wholesomeness and her ordinariness.

1. Look through the four texts and find five nouns or noun phrases used to describe the person.
2. Write them down.

* **Adjectives, nouns and noun phrases**
If you want a quick reminder about all of these, look on pages 157–160.

Darcey Bussell

Bussell has been Britain's biggest dance celebrity since being plucked from the Corps de Ballet at the age of 18. Bussell is known for her wholesomeness and her ordinariness. She giggles in rehearsals, often changes in the same room as the junior dancers and is called Darce by everyone in the company.

Now 28, she's been awarded an OBE, has her painting in the National Portrait Gallery and has even appeared on *French & Saunders*. She has just one failing. According to her friends, when they go to clubs she's surprisingly useless on the dance floor.

Tom Cruise

He could never be dismissed as just another pretty face. Cruise, who earns more than $20 million a movie, is the most powerful actor in the American film industry.

At 35, he combines good looks, respected acting skills and a proven record as the biggest box-office draw in the business. He's made nearly 20 films in 15 years, most of them hits, but you won't find the actor sitting back in satisfaction.

Cruise, a Scientologist who once considered becoming a priest, is a driven man who likes a challenge. He has often avoided easy roles that only need his good looks and toothy grin, and doesn't mind if he appears on screen looking less than lovely.

'I give it everything,' he says. 'There's no middle ground for me.'

Exercise C

Gofer has never heard of any of these people! He wants Yuri to make a programme about people who are 'really famous'. Who do you think would be suitable celebrities for Yuri's programme?

1. Make a list of *five* suitable celebrities.
2. For each one write a sentence explaining why that person is famous.
3. For each one write one or two sentences explaining why that person would be good to interview.
4. You should have written at least ten sentences. Go through them and put a circle round all the adjectives you have used.
5. Underline any noun phrases you have used.

Introducing prepositions

What's wrong?

Yuri keeps making mistakes in his English. There are six mistakes in what he says here.

1. What are the words he has used wrongly?
2. What should he have said in each case?

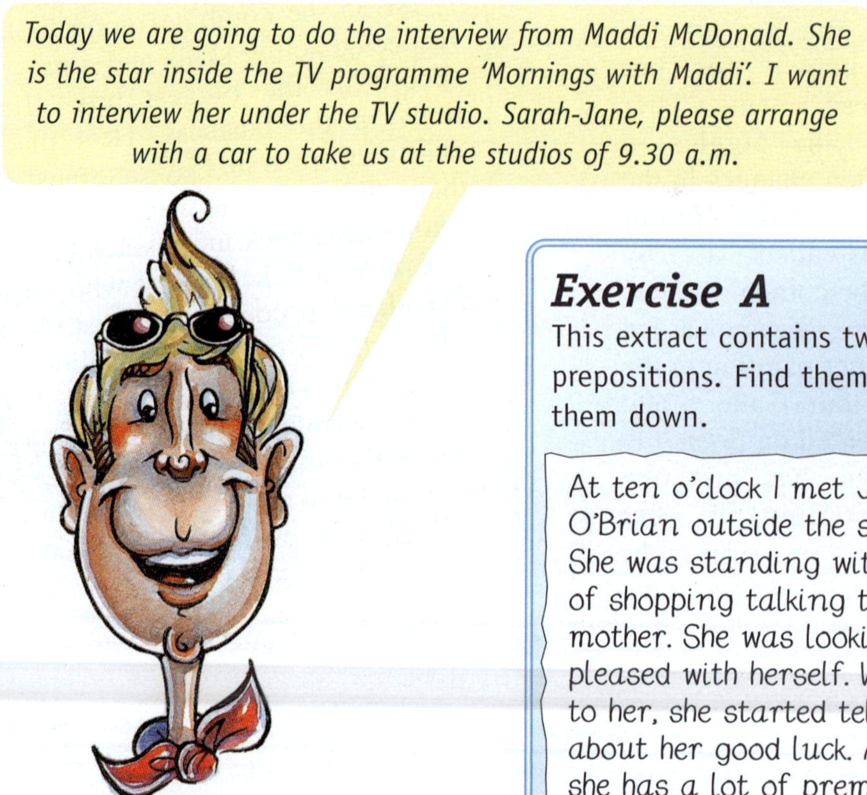

Prepositions

The words that Yuri has been getting wrong are called **prepositions**. These are some of the commonest prepositions:

about	*after*	*at*	*before*
between	*by*	*during*	*for*
from	*in*	*into*	*of*
on	*outside*	*over*	*through*
to	*under*	*up*	*with*
within	*without*		

Exercise A

This extract contains twelve prepositions. Find them and write them down.

> At ten o'clock I met Jasmine O'Brian outside the supermarket. She was standing with a bag full of shopping talking to her mother. She was looking rather pleased with herself. When I spoke to her, she started telling me about her good luck. Apparently she has a lot of premium bonds that she was given by her grandfather. While she was at school today a letter came for her, saying that she had won £10,000!

Exercise B

Choose five prepositions from the list on the left. Write a sentence for each, using it correctly.

What do prepositions do?

They are called 'prepositions' because they are **positioned** before ('**pre**'):

- a noun (e.g. 'after school')
- a pronoun (e.g. 'before you')
- a noun phrase (e.g. 'inside the white room').

The group of words that is formed like this is called a **prepositional phrase**. Prepositional phrases can give us different kinds of information, but many of them answer one of the questions on the right:

Where?

For example: ***behind the tree***

When?

For example: ***after school***

How?

For example: ***by skilful play***

Exercise A

In each of the following sentences a prepositional phrase has been printed in **bold type**. Say which of the three questions above it answers.

1. I left home **at about three o'clock.**
2. I found the missing key **behind my desk.**
3. It fitted the lock and I opened the door **without difficulty.**
4. There is a fierce dog **in the garden next door.**
5. It frightens me **with its fierce bark.**
6. It is always tied **to a post.**
7. I am frightened that it will break its lead and jump **over the fence.**

Exercise B

In each of these sentences there is a blank with one of the three questions in brackets. Make up a prepositional phrase to fill the blank and answer the question. Underline the preposition.

Example:

My birthday is the day _(when?)_.

Answer:

***after*** ***tomorrow***

1. Sam caught the bus _(where?)_.
2. Sam caught the bus _(when?)_.
3. Petra cut her finger _(how?)_.
4. There wasn't much room but I just managed to squeeze _(where?)_.
5. _(when?)_ they're going to the pictures.

Celebrity inventor

Exercise A

In this extract some of the prepositions have been removed. Look at each blank and work out the preposition that should go in it. Write the number of the blank and the preposition you have chosen.

Ben Thompson was a teacher who escaped ___1___ school. He was born ___2___ the United States and besides being a teacher, he was a gymnast and a medical student. Until the war. The American colonists were fighting ___3___ their independence from Britain. But which side should Ben choose? The Americans or the British?

Rumour has it that he chose both. He spied ___4___ the British and the Americans. He was a sort of a double agent. But the British never knew this and King George III gave Ben a knighthood when the war was over.

But Ben liked the excitement of being ___5___ war. He said he didn't want to 'vegetate in England'. So what did he do? Simple! He went ___6___ Bavaria as a special adviser ___7___ War to the government and became Minister for War in 1793.

Exercise B

In this section some prepositional phrases are missing. Work out what you think each one should be. Write the number of each blank and the phrase that should go in it.

As Minister ___8___, Ben devised a cunning plan. The streets were full of beggars and the army was short ___9___. Ben's idea was to force the beggars to make uniforms. But how should he feed the beggars? After much research Ben found the cheapest food was watery vegetable soup. So he 'vegetated' in Bavaria instead of ___10___ – ha, ha. Ben was so keen on this idea he even published a book ___11___. Could this be a new line in school dinners? Then he had a second brainwave. He put soldiers to work growing potatoes to make the soup to feed the beggars who made their uniforms.

Celebrity know-all

Yuri wants to begin his celebrity programme with some odd celebrities from the past. He has asked you to write a short account of a famous nineteenth-century know-all, Baron Lubbock. The extract below gives the information you will need, but some of the words have been missed out.

Exercise A

1. Use the information in the picture book to write between six and ten sentences about Baron Lubbock.
2. When you have finished make a list of the prepositions you used in your sentences.

Celebrity profile

When you worked on page 21, you made a list of celebrities you thought Yuri should include in his programme. Now Yuri has asked you help write the script for the programme. He wants you to write a paragraph about your chosen celebrity. It will be spoken as the first pictures of your celebrity are shown on the screen.

Exercise A

1. Look back at the list you made for Exercise C on page 21.
2. Choose one of the celebrities in your list.
3. Write a **lead sentence** summing up what you think of the person you have chosen.

Exercise B

4. Make a list of five reasons for your opinion about the person – and why you think they are famous.
5. Don't bother to write full sentences – just make sure you get down the important points.

Exercise C

6. Look carefully at the notes you have made. Use them to help you write three or four sentences for the **body of the paragraph**.

Exercise D

7. Now look carefully at the sentences you have written so far. Think carefully about how you can round this paragraph off.
8. Write a **concluding sentence**.

Exercise E

9 Read through all five or six sentences and think about the answers to these questions:

- Does the **lead sentence** really tell people what the paragraph is about?
- Does the **body of the paragraph** build on the lead sentence?
- Do I need to add any sentences?
- Does the **concluding sentence** round the paragraph off properly?

Rewrite your paragraph making any changes you think are needed.

Why we use paragraphs

We organize writing into paragraphs for these reasons:

- It helps us as we write, because it makes us group together sentences about the same topic.
- It makes us think about the best order for our sentences.
- It breaks our writing into sections which make life easier for the reader.

Parts of a paragraph

The lead sentence

This is the first or second sentence of the paragraph. It tells us what the paragraph is going to be about.

The body of the paragraph

This is a group of sentences that follow the lead sentence – and tell the reader more about the subject.

The concluding sentence

This is the last sentence in the paragraph. It sums up what you have said in the paragraph and rounds it off.

Summing up what you've learned

The words we use

When we write about a subject we can choose words which show our feelings about it. In particular we can choose adjectives and nouns that show whether we like or dislike the person or thing we are writing about.

For example, words like:

fearsome	*successful*	*powerful*
respected	*stylish*	*tough*
self-composed		

can show that the writer likes and admires the person being described.

Writing a paragraph

When you are writing in paragraphs, follow these rules:

1. Make sure that each paragraph is about one topic – one part of the whole subject you are writing about.
2. Begin with a **lead sentence** that tells the reader what the paragraph is about.
3. Follow this with a group of sentences that build up information and ideas about the topic. This is the **body of the paragraph**.
4. End each paragraph with a **concluding sentence** that completes the topic in some way.

Prepositions

Common **prepositions** are:

about	*after*	*at*
before	*between*	*by*
during	*for*	*from*
in	*into*	*of*
on	*outside*	*over*
through	*to*	*under*
up	*with*	*within*
without		

Prepositions come before:

- a noun (e.g. 'after school')
- a pronoun (e.g. 'before you')
- a noun phrase (e.g. 'inside the white room').

The group of words that is formed like this is called a **prepositional phrase**. Many prepositional phrases answer one of these questions:

Where? When? How?

Remember, remember …

Every year we celebrate the 5th of November. But how much do you know about the story behind it – the story that 'shall never be forgot'?

- How would you explain it to Yuri?
- What are the important things about the story?
- Why do we still remember it in this particular way?

In this unit you will learn about:

Different ways of telling the same story

Adverbials that tell us about:

- where
- when
- how.

Writing paragraphs and linking them together

The Gunpowder Plot 1605

Gofer came back with several history books. The text that follows is what the team found in one of them.

Laws against Catholics in England had been harsh during Elizabeth I's reign. They had been fined for not going to church, and were not allowed to hold their own services. When James became king, he made vague promises about giving the Catholics freedom to worship as they wanted.

But the king never kept his promise. He knew that most people would protest at a move to help the Catholics. Instead, his chief minister, Robert Cecil, made the penalties more severe. He increased the fines and banished all Catholic priests.

In 1604, a group of Catholics plotted their revenge. They were led by Robert Catesby. Their plan had two parts. First, they would blow up the House of Lords on 5 November 1605. This was the opening day of Parliament, when MPs, the Lords, and the king himself would be there. Secondly, they would start a Catholic rising in the Midlands and drive James from the throne.

The plotters hired a building next to Parliament and tried to dig a tunnel beneath the House of Lords. But the walls were too thick. Then they rented the cellar under the House. Here, they stored about thirty barrels of gunpowder.

The plotters hid the barrels of gunpowder under piles of firewood. One of them, Guy Fawkes, stayed on guard. He was a fanatical Catholic who had been a captain in the Spanish army.

Eight other men joined in the plot. But this brought disaster. One of the new men had a brother-in-law, Lord Monteagle, who would be in Parliament when the barrels exploded. He sent Monteagle a warning letter in code. Monteagle showed the letter to Robert Cecil, who told the king. So, on the night of 4 November, search parties went to the House. They found the gunpowder and arrested Guy Fawkes. Three days later the rest of the plotters were caught by Cecil's men. Catesby and three others were killed. The remaining eight were put in prison, and executed in 1606.

Exercise A

Yuri says, 'Just give the facts! I want answers to these questions – and not, please, more than two sentences for each – one if possible!'

1. Why did these Catholics plot against the king?
2. What did they want to do to the House of Lords?
3. What did they plan to do after that?
4. How were they found out?
5. Where does this Guy Fawkes come into it?

Gunpowder, treason ... and lies?

Another book told the story in a different way.

Everybody knows about Guy Fawkes … or do they? Test your teacher with these well known 'facts' about Guy Fawkes and the Gunpowder Plot. How many are true and how many false?

1 Guy Fawkes was born a Catholic.
2 Guy Fawkes was the leader of the gunpowder plot.
3 Luckily, Guy Fawkes was caught just before he blew up James and his Parliament.
4 Guy Fawkes was tortured and betrayed his friends.

Answers: False! False! False! Oh, and… false!

Here's how …

1 Guy (or Guido as he was christened) was brought up a Protestant. When he was ten his new stepfather (Denis Bainbridge) taught him to follow the Catholic religion. The Catholics had already tried to dispose of Elizabeth I (with a little help from foreign friends, Armadas and poisonous plots). James was just another Protestant monarch to be disposed of … nothing personal!

2 The leader of the Gunpowder Plot was Robert Catesby. Guy was fighting as a soldier for the Spanish army when the plot was first dreamt up. He was smuggled back into England to help – probably because he was an explosives expert.

3 Guy was caught at least 12 hours before Parliament was due to meet the king. And it wasn't 'luck'. The soldiers who caught Guy had been tipped off and were searching for explosives when they found him there. King James had also been tipped off. He was never in any real danger from the Gunpowder Plot.

4 Guy was tortured on the rack for two days before he even gave his real name. It took another two days before he confessed to the plot then *six* more days before he named any other plotters. But, by that time, his partners had already been hunted and arrested or killed. They *had* been betrayed … but not by Guy Fawkes.

Exercise A

This extract and the one on page 30 come from history books.

1. Are they both written for the same kind of reader? If not, what kind of reader is each written for?
2. How would you describe the way in which each one tells the story?
3. Which is easier to read and why?

When, where and how?

Adverbials

In sentences, words and phrases that answer the questions 'When?', 'Where?' and 'How' are called **adverbials**.

***When** did the Gunpowder Plot happen?*
***How** did they try to blow up the House of Lords?*
***Where** did they catch Guy Fawkes?*

*It happened **in 1605**.*
*They tried to blow up the House of Lords **with gunpowder**.*
*They caught Guy Fawkes **underneath the House of Lords**.*

An adverbial can be one word or a group of words, a phrase, like *with gunpowder*. Sometimes it is a phrase starting with a preposition: *underneath the House of Lords*.

Exercise A

Each of these sentences contains an adverbial. For each one, write down the adverbial and say which of the three questions it answers.

1. At last Petra finished her homework.
2. Yesterday we had a holiday.
3. They live in Birmingham.
4. He spoke angrily.
5. Pete reached his home at 5.30.
6. There was a fire down by the supermarket.
7. The parcel was tied with string.

Exercise B

Each of these sentences is followed by a question. Add an adverbial to the sentence in answer to the question.

Example: ***They left.*** (When?)
Answer: ***They left at five o'clock.***

1. Sam won the race. (How?)
2. Our dog was stolen. (When?)
3. There are two new pupils. (Where?)
4. The mother spoke to her child. (How?)
5. Are you going? (Where?)

More about adverbials

Just one word

Often an adverbial is just one word.
A one-word adverbial is an **adverb**.

When?

now	*then*	*later*
today	*tomorrow*	*yesterday*

Where?

here	*there*	*everywhere*
nowhere	*above*	*below*

How?

well	*badly*	*easily*
fast	*slowly*	*angrily*

A group of words

An adverbial can also be a group of words.

When?

in a few days' time
at the end of last week

Where?

beside the tree
above my head

How?

with a piece of string
in a lazy way

Exercise A

Fill the gap in each of these sentences with a single-word adverbial (an adverb). For each one say which of the three questions the adverb provides an answer to.

1. ______ we had the school swimming competition.
2. Dan won the 50 metres freestyle ______.
3. Mark came in ______.
4. ______ we had the medley relay race.
5. ______ Dan swam the breaststroke.
6. ______ Mark swam the backstroke.
7. ______ Martin swam the crawl.
8. All three worked ______.
9. Later Minnie Jones fell ______.
10. Martin pulled her ______.

Exercise B

Fill the gap in each of the sentences from Exercise A with an adverbial that is a group of words. For each one say which of the three questions the adverbial answers.

Civil War adverbials

The texts on these two pages are all about the English Civil war (1642–1649).

Exercise A

In this extract some of the adverbials have been missed out. Each gap contains one of the three questions, *when*, *where* and *how*. The adverbials that fit the gaps and answer the questions are listed below, but in the wrong order. Write the number of each gap and the adverbial that should go in it.

Adverbials

easily *in 1644*
on the edge of a river
out of the town
right round Nantwich
with the Roundheads

King Charles's army suffered from having some dim-witted generals. 1 (when?) Lord Byron took charge of some fresh troops from Ireland and surrounded the Roundhead town of Nantwich. No Roundhead could get 2 (where?) because Lord Byron's troops made a circle 3 (where?) even though the town was 4 (where?) ! It was icy weather. The river was frozen. Brilliant Byron's troops could cross it when they liked. Surely Nantwich would surrender? But … *the ice melted*. The troops across the river were cut off, and Byron's two half-armies were 5 (how?) defeated. Just to make things worse, bird-brain Byron's fed-up Irish troops agreed to switch sides and fight 6 (how?) .

Exercise B

In this section there are no questions to help you. Write the number of the blank, the adverbial that should go in it, and the question it answers.

Adverbials

by the pike men
even worse
forward
in their own ditches
towards him
by the ditch
behind a deep ditch and rows of foot-soldiers with pikes

Lord Byron managed to do 7 at the next battle – Marston Moor, in Yorkshire. He sat with his horse-soldiers (cavalry) 8 . All he had to do was wait for the order and attack the Roundheads. Then he saw the Roundheads coming 9 . They would be slowed up 10 and battered 11 . All he had to do was *wait*. He couldn't. He charged 12 . First he flattened his own pike soldiers, then he got his own men tangled 13 where the Roundheads were able to cut them to pieces. The battle was lost and with it the whole of northern England. All because Lord Byron couldn't wait.

Exercise C

This exercise works in the same way, except that you are not always given the complete missing adverbials:

Clues

honourably – prisoners of war	*1644*
Colchester Castle	*the castle*
Marston Moor	*midnight*
moonlight	*out*
prison	*3 months*

In 1643 a group of London women surrounded the Houses of Parliament shouting, 'Peace and the King.' They were asked to leave. They refused and started beating up Members of Parliament – especially the crop-haired Puritans. In the end the army was called in to drive them __14__. Three women were killed and many others locked __15__.

The Cavalier leader, Prince Rupert, also came face to face with the Roundheads __16__, __17__. By the time he reached the battlefield there was just an hour of daylight left. Hardly worth starting a battle now, he thought. So he ordered his men to stop and have supper. The Roundheads couldn't believe what they were seeing. While the Cavaliers were having a bite to eat the Roundheads attacked and massacred 3,000 of them. They fought on __18__ and __19__ the Cavaliers had lost the battle.

The Cavalier town of Colchester, Essex, was under siege in 1648. The siege went on __20__ and the inhabitants were forced to eat cats and dogs. It got worse. When they heard that Cromwell was winning the war, they gave up. The leaders expected to be treated __21__. The Roundheads took them __22__ and shot them. (Maybe they were cat-lovers.)

The Parliament forces had problems too. Beeston Castle was left in the care of a Parliament commander whose peace-time work was selling cheese. One night a Cavalier officer and eight men climbed the rock that the castle was built upon and crept __23__. The cheese-seller was so shocked he surrendered his 60 men … and then invited the attackers to supper and a drink of beer. When the angry Roundheads caught up with the cowardly cheese-seller, they shot him.

Celebrating Guy Fawkes Night

Sarah-Jane has asked you to help her write the commentary for the film describing Bonfire Night and explaining why people celebrate it. This film is being made for people in Yuri's country who don't know anything about Guy Fawkes or Bonfire Night. He wants to give them information but he also wants them to be entertained and enjoy the programme.

Sarah-Jane wants you to write about four things:

1. a description of what people do on Bonfire Night
2. how this goes back to something that happened in the seventeenth century and why Catholics plotted against the king
3. what the plotters planned to do
4. the part that Guy Fawkes played in it.

(If you can't remember all the details, you can look again at pages 30 and 31.)

Exercise A

Begin by writing a paragraph about what people do on Bonfire Night.

1. Make a list of four or five key points that you want to mention. For example, these might include making a guy, fireworks, the bonfire, and what people eat and drink.
2. Think of a good sentence to start the paragraph – the **lead sentence**.
3. Then write three or four sentences covering the other points in your list – the **body** of the paragraph.
4. Think of a sentence that will round off what you have written – a **concluding sentence**.

Exercise B

Now do the same for the other points in the list at the bottom of page 36. Write one paragraph for each one, following the guidelines in Exercise A.

Exercise C

You should now have a **first draft** of four paragraphs. As you wrote them, you were concentrating on each paragraph separately. Now you have to make them fit together. A good way to do this is to make sure that the last sentence of one paragraph links with the first sentence of the next. Like this:

> Laws against Catholics in England had been harsh during Elizabeth I's reign. They had been fined for not going to church, and were not allowed to hold their own services. **When James became king, he made vague promises about giving the Catholics freedom to worship as they wanted.**
>
> **But the king never kept his promise.** He knew

Go through your first draft making changes, so that it flows from one paragraph to the next, like the example.

Summing up what you've learned

Same subject, different ways of writing

Two people can write about the same subject in different ways, even when they are writing for the same audience:

- They can select different parts of the subject to write about.
- They can write about them in a different order.
- They can use a different **tone of voice**. They can be more formal and serious: 'The king's generals made a number of serious mistakes.' Or they can be less formal and more jokey: 'King Charles's army suffered from having some dim-witted generals.'

Paragraphing

If you write more than a few sentences, you should divide your writing into paragraphs. Each paragraph should have three parts:

- a lead sentence
- the body of the paragraph, made up of from three to five sentences
- a concluding sentence.

When you can, you should make a link between the concluding sentence of one paragraph and the lead sentence of the next.

Adverbials

In sentences, words and phrases that answer the questions 'When?, 'Where?' and 'How' are called **adverbials**. In these examples the adverbials are underlined.

It happened <u>in 1605</u>. (When)
They tried to blow up the House of Lords <u>with gunpowder</u>. (How)
They caught Guy Fawkes <u>underneath the House of Lords</u>. (Where)

Just one word

Often an adverbial is just one word.

When?

now	*then*	*later*
today	*tomorrow*	*yesterday*

Where?

here	*there*	*everywhere*
nowhere	*above*	*below*

How?

well	*badly*	*easily*
fast	*slowly*	*angrily*

A group of words

An adverbial can also be a group of words.

When?
in a few days' time
at the end of last week
Where?
beside the tree
above my head
How?
with a piece of string
in a lazy way

UNIT 4

Follow the instructions

Yuri is still having problems with English. He understands most of what he hears and reads but he often misses some of the details.

- In what kinds of situation do you have to read instructions and follow them?
- Do you ever find it difficult to follow instructions?
- If so, what makes it difficult?

In this unit you will learn about:

Instructions:

- different kinds of writing for different readers
- how pictures are used.

Adverbs:

- for 'When?', 'Where?' and 'How?'
- working with adjectives and other adverbs to make phrases.

Writing and drafting:

- how to write clear and simple instructions.

Words and pictures

Yuri is trying to improve his English by learning how to read instructions. He has borrowed a book from the library about how to make simple games. Unfortunately someone has torn some of the pages out. This page and the one on page 41 obviously don't go together!

Making a Draught Board

You will need:

hard white card
ruler
pencil
scissors
black pen

1 Draw a square that is 30cm × 30cm on a piece of hard white card. Cut it out.

2 Take a ruler and place it on the edge of the square with the zero on the edge of the board. Working along the ruler put a small mark in pencil every 2.5cm on the board.

3 Now do the same for the other three sides of the square.

4 Using your ruler, draw straight lines between the marks on opposite sides of the board.

5 Take a black pen and colour the first square in one corner of the board black. Then colour every alternate square on the board black.

Exercise A

There should be a picture page to go with these instructions. Can you help Yuri by telling him what should be in the illustrations?

1. Work out how many pictures each instruction needs.
2. Give each one a letter. So if instruction number 1 needs two pictures, call them 1a and 1b. Then the pictures for instruction number 2 will be 2a and 2b – and so on.
3. Write a short description of what should be in each picture.
4. Choose one of the instructions and draw the pictures that should go with it.

Making a Game of Solitaire

You will need:

heavy card
soup plate
32 acorns, hazel nuts or marbles
compass
pencil
knife
scissors
ruler
paint
paint brush

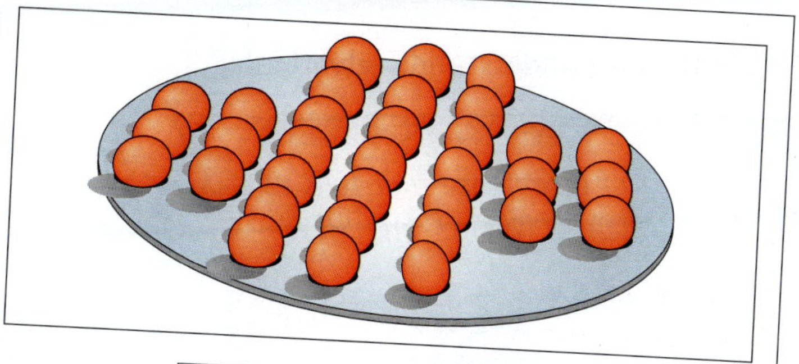

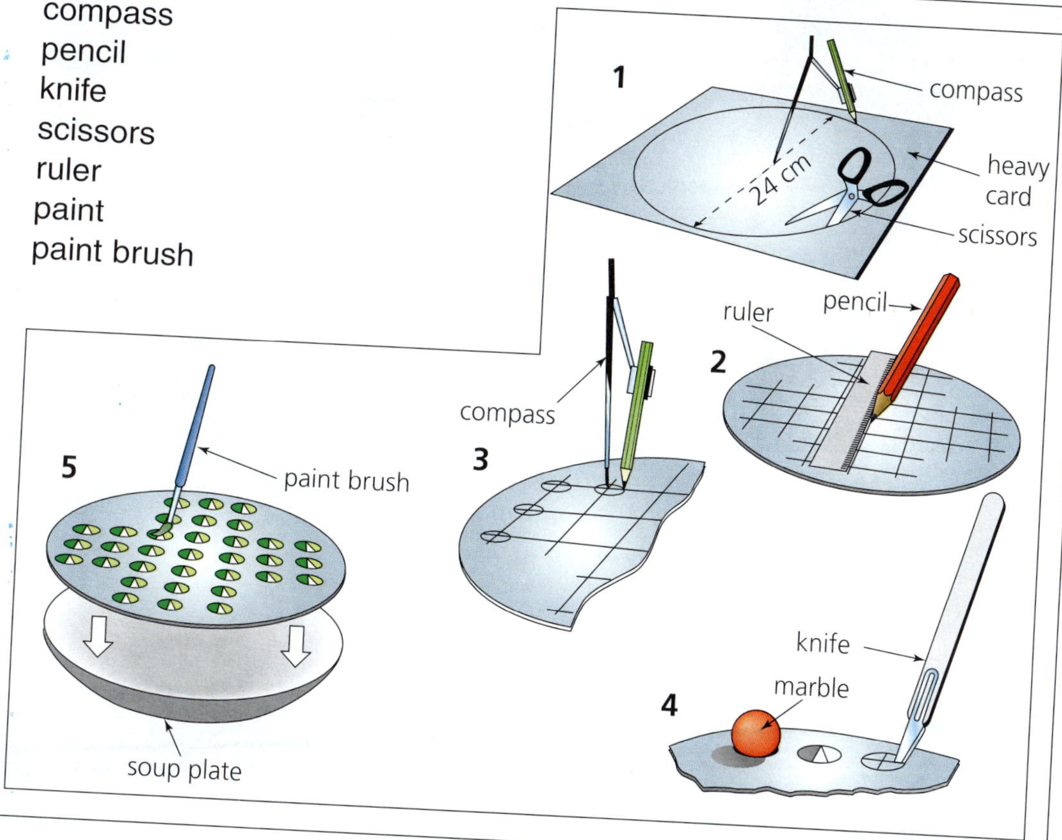

Exercise B

There should be an instruction page to go with these pictures. Can you help Yuri by telling him what should be in the instructions?

1. Look at the pictures and the 'You will need' list. Make sure that you understand what is being shown in each picture.
2. Work out how to make the game.
3. Look at picture 1. Write clear instructions to go with it.
4. Do the same thing for all the other pictures.

Adverbials and adverbs

Yuri thinks he understands adverbials.

Who is right?

They both are. An adverbial can be a group of words or a single word:

When?	**Where?**	**How?**
now	***here***	***easily***
at the moment	***in this area***	***without any difficulty***

Adverbs

These words are **adverbs**:

When?	***now***	***then***	***yesterday***
Where?	***here***	***there***	***behind***
How?	***slowly***	***well***	***dangerously***

Exercise A

Each of these sentences contains one adverb. Write it down and say which of the three questions on page 42 it answers.

1. She was standing there.
2. Peter spoke excitedly.
3. Come here!
4. That dog runs fast.
5. It happened today.
6. It was raining hard.
7. He put it down.
8. Move on, please.
9. They were behaving badly.
10. Do it now!

Making adverbs out of adjectives

Many adjectives can be made into adverbs by adding **-ly**.

sad + ly = sadly
easy + ly = easily
skilful + ly = skilfully

Words that end in -ly

As you have seen, a lot of adverbs end in **-ly**. But beware!

1. Some words that end in **-ly** are not adverbs; for example, *friendly*, *silly* and *cowardly*. We don't usually turn these into adverbs by adding **-ly**. Instead we use a phrase. For example:
   She was behaving in a silly way.
2. Some adverbs do not end in *-ly*.

Exercise B

1. Make each of these adjectives into an adverb. Make sure that you have got the spelling right! (Look at the rule at the bottom of the page.)
   clever extreme happy
   fearful bright
2. For each of the adverbs you have made, say which of the three questions it answers.

Exercise C

Look at Exercise A. Find five adverbs that do not end in **-ly**.

Spelling rule: adding -ly

Just add **-ly** to the adjective. Exceptions:

1. If the word ends in **-ll**, just add **-y**: *full* → *fully*.
2. If the word ends in **-y**, change the **y** to an **i**: *messy* → *messily*.

Using adverbs

Exercise A

In this extract some of the adverbs have been missed out. Write down the number of each blank and a suitable adverb to fill it, chosen from the list below.

Adverbs

literally	*never*
only	*rather*
somehow	*sometimes*
unconsciously	*unexpectedly*
usually	*very*

To those familiar with his strange talents, Chris Robinson is known as the dream detective. The 46-year-old psychic lives in Bedfordshire, England, and claims to ___1___ dream the future.

Every night while Chris sleeps, he keeps a blank pad of paper and a pen by his bedside. While he is asleep and dreaming, he scribbles down notes, ___2___ writing down what he is seeing and what is happening in the dreams. ___3___, if the dream was vivid, Chris will be able to remember it when he wakes up. On other occasions he has only the notes in his dream diary to go on. The dreams that Chris has can be ___4___ complex and ___5___ need what he calls 'decoding' by him the next day.

Exercise B

In this part of the story more adverbs have been removed, but no help is given. Write the number of each blank and a suitable adverb to fill it.

In November 1991, Chris began to dream about a terrorist attack on the town of St Albans in Hertfordshire near where he lives. The dreams contained the postcode for St Albans. Chris saw the two terrorists walk down the high street in St Albans carrying a bomb in a large envelope. Just as they pushed it through the letterbox of a bank, it exploded, killing them both and destroying the bank. For several nights running, Chris dreamt of bombs in St Albans, ___6___ a sign that the attack would happen ___7___ soon. Chris got in touch with his police contacts. 'By now they were listening to what I had to say. What I did not know was that an army band was due to play in the public hall near the bank on the night I predicted the attack would happen. The police took my warning ___8___ and that night they had extra surveillance keeping watch on the area.'

Two of the surveillance officers on the roof of a main-street store saw a suspicious-looking pair of people walking towards the bank and reported it. The concert was about to end, but rather than take a chance, the band was told to keep playing and the crowd was kept ___9___. It was just as well.

As the pair of terrorists put the bomb through the letter box of the bank, it exploded – killing them both ___10___ as it had happened in Chris's dream. If the crowd had been coming out of the hall at that moment, many of them would have died as well.

Words and phrases

We have seen that one important job adverbs do is as the adverbial in a sentence, answering the questions 'When?', 'Where?' and 'How?'.

Exercise A

Each of these sentences contains an adverb in **bold** type. Rewrite the sentence replacing the adverb with a phrase that has a similar meaning.

Example: Draw round the plate *carefully*.

Answer: Draw round the plate *with great care*.

1. The car travelled **fast** along the open road.
2. Teresa wrote **thoughtfully.**
3. Martin answered the question **hesitantly.**
4. The speaker droned on **monotonously.**
5. The ball trickled **feebly** between the posts.

Exercise B

Each of these sentences contains a phrase in **bold** type. Rewrite the sentence replacing the phrase with an adverb that has a similar meaning.

Example: ***Draw round the plate*** ***with great care*.**

Answer: ***Draw round the plate*** ***carefully*.**

6. The meeting took place **behind closed doors.**
7. They entered the house **without a sound.**
8. It happened **without any warning.**
9. Peter opened the box **by brute force.**
10. These machines cannot be operated **by hand.**

A choice of adverbs

The phrase *with great care* can be replaced by these adverbs:

carefully
cautiously
thoroughly
precisely
accurately

Exercise C

Write down all the adverbs you can think of to replace each of these phrases:

11. with intelligence
12. by good fortune
13. on and on
14. without being seen

Writing instructions

On pages 40 and 41 we looked at some of the different ways in which people write instructions. Now it's your turn. Follow the guidelines on this page and the next to write a set of instructions.

Exercise A: Prepare

1. Write down the **subject** of your instructions. Choose one of the following suggestions or think of a topic of your own:
   - how to make a folded paper model
   - how to make a game
   - how to play a game
   - how to make a simple toy.
2. Write down the **audience** you are going to write for. (For example, is it people of your age, young children or adults?)
3. Write one or two sentences explaining any **background knowledge** you expect them to have (for example, any special words you expect them to understand).

Exercise B: Plan

4. Make a list of:
   - **equipment or tools** needed
   - **materials** needed.
5. Make a list of the **stages** you have to go through. Check that:
   - you haven't missed any out
   - they are in the right order.

Exercise C: Write the first draft

Before you start, rule a line down the middle of the page. Write your first draft to the left of it. Leave the right-hand side empty.

6. Write a short paragraph introducing your instructions:
   - Tell your reader what you are going to explain.
   - Include the list of equipment and materials you made in Exercise B.
   - Explain anything else readers need to understand before they begin.
7. Write one paragraph for each of the stages you have in your list.
8. Number your paragraphs.

Exercise D: Edit your draft

Use the right-hand side of the page for rewriting.

9 Now read your first draft and imagine that you are the person it is written for. Imagine that you are reading about this subject for the first time. Look for sentences that are not clear. Write them again.

10 Look for places where you have not written enough and need to explain in more detail. Write the extra sentences you need.

11 Look for places where your sentences are too long or complicated. Make them shorter and easier.

Exercise E: Think about illustrations

12 Look through your first draft again. Look for places where your instructions would be easier if there was a simple diagram. Remember that you have to draw it, so make sure that any diagrams are easy to draw!

13 Make a list of the drawings you need. Write a few words describing what is in each drawing. Keep your list as short as possible.

14 Against each of the drawings write the number of the paragraph it illustrates.

Exercise F: Write the final version

For the final version use a fresh page or sheet of paper.

15 Write each paragraph again using the changes you made in Exercise D.

16 Draw the diagrams as you get to them.

17 When you have finished, check for mistakes in spelling, punctuation and grammar.

Summing up what you've learned

Adverbs

Adverbs are a class of words – like nouns and adjectives. They can be the adverbial in a sentence, answering the questions:

- Where? *I walked there.*
- When? *I went yesterday.*
- How? *I walked slowly.*

Making adverbs from adjectives

Most adjectives can be made into adverbs by adding **-ly**:

sad + ly = sadly
easy + ly = easily
skilful + ly = skilfully

But not all adverbs end in **-ly** (for example, *fast*, *never*, *there*). And some words that end in **-ly** are not adverbs. For example, *silly*, *friendly* and *cowardly* are all adjectives – and you cannot turn these into adverbs by adding **-ly**.

Extra information about adverbs

Adverbs can work with adjectives. We say that they **modify** the adjectives:

- *It was a fairly exciting film.*
- *It was a very exciting film.*
- *It was a fantastically exciting film.*

They can also modify adverbs. For example:

- *quite quickly*
- *incredibly quickly.*

Writing instructions

The audience

When you write instructions you have to think very carefully about your readers. Think about:

1. what background information they may need
2. special words that may need explaining
3. (if they are young children) how well they can read.

Planning

You should plan writing carefully:

1. List all materials and equipment needed.
2. List the stages in note form.
3. Check the stages and make sure that you haven't missed any out and that they are in the right order.

Drafting

Write an introductory paragraph and then one paragraph for each stage.

Checking and rewriting

Make sure that you go through your draft and check that it is clear and easy to understand. If possible get someone else to read it and comment on it. Make any changes that are needed and then make a fair copy.

Revision unit

The theme of this unit is 'Winter Festivals'. It is mainly a revision unit. In it you will go back over some of the work you have done in Units 1–4. Yuri is making a programme about the different religious celebrations that happen in the winter. As you work through the unit you will read about Christian, Jewish and Hindu festivals that are celebrated at this time throughout the world.

In this unit you will revise:

- sentence complements
- prepositions
- adverbials
- adverbs
- paragraphing.

Revising complements and objects

Exercise A

In this extract eight phrases are printed in **bold**.

- Five are objects.
- Three are complements.

Write down the number of each phrase and then whether it is an object or a complement.

St Lucia's Day

St Lucia's Day is **13 December (1)**. In Sweden this is like the beginning of Christmas. It is celebrated everywhere: in schools, churches, shops and offices. They have processions where the main girl is dressed as a Lucia queen or bride. She dresses in a long white dress and a red sash. On her head is a crown of evergreen leaves and lighted candles. Other girls also dress in white and hold a candle each. The boys are called **'star boys' (2)**, and they wear cone-shaped hats made from thin cardboard and decorated with paper stars. They all sing **special carols (3)** and give out ginger biscuits. In some churches the choir dresses up for the procession. After the carols, everyone goes to the church hall for coffee and buns.

In Swedish homes it is often the youngest girl who dresses up as St Lucia. She is supposed to make **breakfast in bed (4)** for the rest of the family. They all enjoy **coffee and yellow St Lucia buns (5)**.

Who was St Lucia?

We do not know much about St Lucia. She was **an early Christian martyr (6)**. This means that she died because of her religion. The white dress may stand for her holiness, and the red sash for her death. Many legends have grown up about her. One is that she helped the Christians who were hiding in the tunnels under Rome in Italy. She found **her way through the dark tunnels (7)** by wearing candles on her head, a bit like a miner's torch. Another legend says that at a time of great hunger in Sweden she miraculously appeared and fed **people (8)**.

Exercise B

Write sentences answering these questions:

1. Where does the complement come in a statement sentence?
2. What kind of verb do sentences with complements have? Give an example.
3. How can you tell a complement from an object?

Revising prepositions

Exercise A

In this extract a number of prepositions have been missed out. Write down the number of each blank and the preposition that you think should go in it.

Light and decorations

St Lucia is the patron saint __1__ light, so people celebrate her day __2__ lighting candles. Her saint's day comes __3__ the middle of winter. December is the darkest month __4__ the year in Sweden. Even __5__ the time of Jesus, people celebrated mid-winter festivals __6__ light. They wanted to brighten up the long dark days. They also decorated their homes __7__ evergreens, like holly and fir trees. These things were living when everything else __8__ nature seemed to be dead. They gave them hope that spring would come again __9__ lighter days, and everything would start growing again. Some of these old customs have now become part __10__ Christmas celebrations. There are lots of different lights at Christmas, and people decorate their homes __11__ trees and holly. You will find other Christian customs that started __12__ Christianity. Often they have been given new Christian meanings.

Exercise B

Write the answers to these questions about prepositions:

1. Give five more prepositions that you have not used in Exercise A.
2. The name 'preposition' means 'placed before'. What kinds of word can we place a preposition before? (2 answers)
3. What kind of phrase can we place a preposition before? (1 answer)

Revising adverbials

Exercise A

In this extract four adverbials have been missed out. They are listed on the right, together with some others that do not come from the passage. Write the number of each blank, the adverbial that should go in it, and the question (*Where?*, *When?*, *How?*) that it answers.

Adverbials

around the place
in America
in India and Nepal
in the world
in many different forms
somehow or other
through many gods and goddesses
without thinking about it

Divali

Divali is a Hindu festival celebrated by Hindus wherever they live __1__. (Sikhs also celebrate Divali but for different reasons.) Most Hindus live __2__. Hinduism is one of the world's oldest religions and of all the world's main religions, Hinduism has the third largest number of followers.

One God

Hindus believe that there is one God, one Supreme Being, called Brahman. Hindus also believe that Brahman can be pictured and thought about __3__. This shows the power and presence of God, who is believed to be everywhere. This is why Hindus worship Brahman __4__. The festival of Divali has exciting stories about some of these gods and goddesses.

Exercise B

In this extract four adverbials have been missed out and replaced by a question. There are clues to the answers on the right. Write the number of the question and a suitable adverbial to answer it.

Clues

bright lights
across world
India
families + friends

The meaning of Divali

The name Divali comes from the word *Deepavali*, which means 'row of lights'. Divali is the most widely celebrated festival 5 (Where?), although the celebrations differ from place to place. But there are some things about the festival that are common 6 (Where?). The lighting of lamps, called divas; cleaning, and sometimes painting, homes; feasting 7 (How?); and illuminating homes, shops, streets and public buildings 8 (How?) – these are some of the ways Divali is celebrated by Hindus wherever they live in the world. The festival can last up to five days.

The most important meaning of the festival is the celebration of the triumph of good over evil. It is also a time for renewing hopes for happiness and prosperity in life.

Revising adverbs

Exercise A

In this extract five words are printed in **bold** type. Two of them are adverbs and three belong to other word classes.

1. Write down the two adverbs.
2. Write down the other three words and say which word class they belong to.

In the second century BC, the Israelite Judah Maccabee defeated the Greek **tyrant** who had forced the Jews to abandon their religion. The Temple was re-dedicated, but there was only enough oil for the Temple lamp to last one day, and it would take eight days to prepare a fresh **supply**. The lamp was lit nonetheless, and **miraculously** it kept burning for eight days.

An eight-branched candlestick is lit for the festival, one candle burning on the first day, two on the second, and so on **for** eight days, celebrating the survival of the Jewish faith in adversity. Hanukah is **especially** popular with Jews in Europe and the United States, because it falls at winter holiday times and is celebrated as a children's festival.

Exercise B

Some of these adjectives can be made into adverbs by adding **-ly**. Write down the numbers of those that can and the adverb they make.

1. greedy
2. small
3. thoughtful
4. fast
5. quick
6. friendly
7. easy
8. possible
9. cowardly
10. simple

Exercise C

Choose four of the adverbs you made in Exercise B and write sentences using them correctly.

Christmas in Mexico

Exercise A

This description of Christmas in Mexico has been printed without paragraph breaks. It should be divided into six paragraphs. Work out where each paragraph should begin. Write down the line number and the first three words of the new paragraph.

In Mexico, Christmas is not a season for giving presents but for acting out the Christmas story in a popular way. Celebrations start nine days before December 25. These days are called posadas, the Spanish for 'lodgings'. The word refers to the inns at which Jesus and Mary stopped on their journey to Bethlehem. Each night a family gives their home as a posada for a festive evening. When darkness falls, processions form led by children. They carry a small litter with statues or clay figures of Mary riding on a donkey, Joseph walking in front and an angel following. Everyone else carries a lighted candle and all join in singing hymns. The procession halts at a house with a song asking for hospitality for the divine travellers. With a song in reply they are told that the household is asleep. They are threatened with beating if they stay. They try at other houses till they reach the posada which has been chosen in advance. Here they kneel, sing and place the images on a temporary altar decorated with flowers and tapers. After the adoration ceremony the night's celebrations continue with plenty of Mexican refreshments, music and dancing. Each night of the nine posadas a pinata or clay jar is broken. This can be a jar of any size, covered with bright-coloured papier mâché figures such as aeroplanes, birds, animals or even Donald Ducks. It contains sweets and toys. In rich homes, pinatas may also hold silk stockings and jewellery. Children are blindfolded, given a stick and have to find and break a pinata which two people hold dangling from a rope. Usually the youngest child is allowed to break it and everybody scrambles for its contents. On Christmas Eve the images are taken to a crib where the Christ Child is venerated. After Midnight Mass bells are rung, whistles blown and fireworks set off.

Words from different languages

Yuri has noticed that the English language contains words that have been taken from many different countries and cultures. He has started making a list. See if you can help him by copying and completing this table:

Word	Country/Area	Meaning/Clue
	Middle East	part of maths that uses 'x's and 'y's
boomerang		
broccoli		
brochure	France	
	India/Pakistan	single-storey house
cotton	Middle East	
		hot spicy food
juggernaut	India/Pakistan	
jungle		
macaroni		
meringue		
outback		
		spaghetti and lasagne are both types of this
	Italy	large musical instrument with keys
pizza		
	France	place where you can buy a meal
vehicle	France	
verandah		
walkabout		
wallaby		

Celebrating the winter festival

Yuri is collecting personal accounts of how people celebrate their winter festival – whether it is Christmas, Divali, Hanukah, or some other celebration that falls at this time of the year. Tell him how you celebrate this season and what you think of it.

Exercise A

Write a paragraph describing how you celebrate the season.

Exercise B

Write a second paragraph explaining what you think are the good things about this celebration (and the bad ones, if you think there are any).

UNIT 6

Flooded!

Yuri is making a programme about winter storms and floods.

If Yuri interviewed you, how would you answer these questions?

- What would you say is typical winter weather in the place where you live?
- Do you like or dislike the winter?
- Why?

What do you think Yuri should include in his programme about winter weather?

In this unit you will learn about:

Looking at texts:

- stories, descriptions, explanations and arguments
- how language has changed over time.

Verbs:

- main verbs and auxiliary verbs
- the five forms of a verb.

Vocabulary:

- choosing weather verbs.

Writing:

- using paragraphs
- writing about weather and storms.

The storm of 1987

Yuri has been collecting information about winds and storms. He needs help in understanding them. Read the texts and then look at the exercise at the bottom of the page.

A

A fierce storm travelling up the coast of western Europe strengthened as it blew northwards. By 1 a.m. on 16 October, high winds were sweeping across northern France. As the winds increased to hurricane force, with gusts of up to 215 kilometres per hour, the storm crossed the English Channel. At 4 a.m., with the wind approaching 160 kilometres (100 miles) per hour, the storm hit London. Roofs were blown off, roads were blocked, trains were cancelled and aircraft were grounded. The hurricane left behind eighteen dead, hundreds of injuries and millions of pounds' worth of damage.

B

Bognor feels the full fury of the gale

Bognor Regis residents woke on Friday to find themselves almost cut off from the outside world with lengthy power and telephone blackouts, roads blocked by trees and no train services.

Arun District Council set up an emergency control centre at its Littlehampton civic offices to handle a constant stream of calls from frantic householders and tree gangs were despatched to help clear roads.

As the full extent of the damage to homes became apparent, homeless people flooded into Bognor police station and Town Hall.

C

Winds are caused by movements of warm and cold air. Warm air is lighter than cold air and so rises, creating an area of low pressure at the Earth's surface. In other places cold air sinks down towards the Earth's surface, and spreads out to create an area of high pressure. Winds are therefore movements of air over the Earth's surface from areas of high pressure to areas of low pressure.

Exercise A

1. **Where** do you think each of these extracts came from? Was it:
   - a book (if so, what kind of book)
   - a newspaper
   - a magazine
   - somewhere else?
2. What kind of writing does each one contain? **How** is it written? Is it:
   - a story
   - a description
   - an explanation
   - an argument?
3. Write an explanation of the meaning of each of these words:
   hurricane ***gust*** ***pressure***

Storms long ago

These extracts are about storms that happened in the past. Read them and then look at the exercise at the bottom of the page.

A

On Friday, the 26th November, in the afternoon, about four of the clock, a country fellow came running to me in a great fright, and very earnestly entreated me to go and see a pillar, as he called it, in the air in a field hard by. I went with the fellow: and when I came, found it to be a spout marching directly with the wind. And I can think of nothing I can compare it to better than the trunk of an elephant, which it resembled, only much bigger. It was extended to a great length, and swept the ground as it went, leaving a mark behind. It crossed a field, and what was very strange . . . meeting with an oak that stood towards the middle of the field, snapped the body of it asunder. Afterwards, crossing a road, it sucked up the water that was in the cart-ruts. Then, coming to an old barn, it tumbled down.

B

At the Government House every precaution was taken to guard against what might happen; the doors and windows were barricaded up, but it availed little. By ten o'clock the wind forced itself a passage through the house from the NNW and, the tempest increasing every minute, the family took to the centre of the building, imagining from the prodigious strength of the walls, they being three feet thick, and from its circular form, it would have withstood the wind's utmost rage: however, by half after eleven o'clock, they were obliged to retreat to the cellar, the wind having forced its way into every part, and torn off most of the roof.

Exercise A

Both these texts were written during the eighteenth century. Since then English has changed in a number of ways.

1. Look through each text and find any words that seem to you old-fashioned. Write them down and beside each one write the word we might use today.
2. Now find three sentences that you think are particularly old-fashioned. Write down the first and last words of them, like this: 'On Friday ... hard by.'
3. Choose one of these sentences and write out what it means in modern English.

How many verb words?

Like many foreign learners of English, Yuri finds our verbs difficult to manage. He thought the verb in a sentence was just one word. Now he finds Sarah-Jane using sentence verbs like 'should have been filming' – four words!

Perhaps you can help him out.

Exercise A

Write down the whole verb in each of these sentences:

1. High winds were sweeping across northern France.
2. The winds increased to hurricane force.
3. Cold air sinks down towards the earth's surface.
4. The tree had fallen to the ground.
5. They had to hide in the cellar.
6. She had to show me the damage.
7. Warm air rises up from the earth's surface.
8. A fierce storm was travelling up the coast of western Europe.
9. The hurricane left behind eighteen dead.
10. The storm had swept across the Channel.

The main verb

Each of the verbs you have written down in Exercise A has one word that means something and one or more that don't seem to have much meaning:

We should have been filming by now.

should have been → NOT MUCH MEANING

filming → PLENTY OF MEANING

When a sentence verb has more than one word, all the words are verbs. The word with the meaning is called the **main verb**. The other words are called **auxiliary verbs**.

Exercise B

Look at the verbs you collected for Exercise A. Copy and complete this table, placing the parts of each verb in the correct column:

	Auxiliary verb(s)	Main verb
1	were	sweeping
2		

What do auxiliary verbs do?

Yuri wants to know what auxiliary verbs *do*. Can you explain? Exercise C shows you one way to do this.

Exercise C

1. In the following sentences the auxiliary verbs have been missed out. There is a blank in each sentence where they should be. For each sentence write down what the auxiliary verb(s) should be.
   - **a** I _______ going home from school when I saw Jamie.
   - **b** We _______ _______ waiting for you for two hours!
   - **c** She _______ going to London on the train tomorrow.
   - **d** Petra and Mark _______ gone home, I'm afraid.
   - **e** They _______ taken their children with them.
2. Explain to Yuri why the auxiliary verbs are needed in these sentences.

List of auxiliary verbs

am *is* *are*
was *were*
has been *have been* *had been*

has *have* *had*

shall *should*
will *would*
can *could*
may *might*
must *ought*

Parts of the main verb

Auxiliary verbs are used with these forms of the main verb:

present participle
walking *going* *blowing*

past participle
walked *gone* *blown*

Using verbs in sentences

Exercise A

In this extract the correct form of some of the verbs has been replaced by the infinitive. Write the number of the blank and the correct form of the verb.

'It began to rain and I __1 (to think)__ I would go home,' said Mrs Cox. 'I __2 (to open)__ the door and saw a great wall that seemed to be smoke, driving in front of it white billows that looked like steam. There was a deep roar, like a train, but many, many times louder.

'The air was full of everything – boards, branches of trees, pans, stoves, all churning around together. I __3 (to see)__ whole sides of houses rolling along near the ground.

'It __4 (to seem)__ to me that I must reach my two children in school, and I opened the door again, bent my head down against the wind and __5 (to start)__ out. Then the storm hit me. I was blown back into the restaurant and against the stove. The building rocked back and forth and then it began to fall in. Fire __6 (to flash)__ in great puffs from the stove.

'I tried to get away from it. I was afraid I would be burned to death. But the wind __7 (to blow)__ me back again against it. Then the walls __8 (to fall)__ in. The roof fell. Something __9 (to hit)__ me on the head.'

Exercise B

In this extract some verbs have been missed out but no help is given. Write down a suitable verb to go in each blank.

'How long I was unconscious I __10__. When I came to I was buried under boards and timbers. Near me was the body of a red cow which seemed to be holding some of the weight off of me.

'Then came Joe Moschenrose, the butcher, looking for his sister. He __11__ me, __12__ some of the heavy boards, __13__ the cow up and __14__ me out. I got up and looked around. There, on the floor, white in death, was Lulu, with a great wound in her head.

'I __15__ for the school. I __16__ my own raincoat down the street hanging on a twisted pile of planking. I __17__ it when the storm struck. I put my hand in the pocket. There was my husband's pay check.

'There was a great crowd about the school. Children were screaming and crying. Mothers and fathers __18__ silently. But everybody __19__ to dig out their own children. I found mine. They were both hurt, but alive.'

Weather verbs

English has plenty of verbs to describe rain, flooding, storms and wind. Sometimes it is difficult to know which one to choose.

Exercise A

These are some of the verbs we can use to describe the action of the wind:

blast	*blow*	*bluster*	*buffet*
gust	*howl*	*moan*	*murmur*
roar	*whisper*	*whistle*	

We can put them into a league table, with the weakest at the top and the strongest at the bottom:

murmur
roar

1. Copy out the table and write in the other words in the order you think is best.
2. Choose three of the words and write a sentence for each one, using it as vividly as you can.

Exercise B

These verbs are all about the action of the sun:

bake	*blaze*	*bleach*	*burn*
dry	*glare*	*glimmer*	*roast*
scorch	*shine*	*toast*	

1. Divide them into two groups:
   a verbs that describe how the sun shines
   b verbs that describe the effect the sun has on things.
2. Make each of your lists into a league table, with the weakest at the top and the strongest at the bottom.
3. Choose two words from each list and write a sentence for each one, using it as vividly as you can.

Exercise C

These verbs describe how rain can fall:

cascade   *drip*   *pour*

1. How many more rain verbs can you think of? Make a list of them.
2. Make your list into a league table, with the weakest at the top and the strongest at the bottom.
3. Choose three words from the list and write a sentence for each one, using it as vividly as you can.

Flooded out!

Yuri is looking for 'human interest' stories about floods. The people who watch his programmes want to know how severe weather affects ordinary people – and how they cope. The pictures on this page tell the story of how one family, Alan and Gemma Willcox and their son Andie, found their home flooded out.

You are going to tell the story of what happened to the Willcoxes in two different ways.

Exercise A

Begin by getting a clear idea of what actually happened.

1. Make a list of the events that are shown in the pictures. Label them, using the letters on the pictures. After you have written about one picture, leave a space of three lines before you write about the next picture.
2. Obviously a lot happened in between the pictures. For example, between pictures F and G the Willcoxes must have been taken somewhere else, where they stayed until the flood waters went down. Use the spaces you have left and describe the other things that must have happened.

Exercise B

Now you are going to tell the story of what happened as if you were Alan or Gemma. Imagine that you are writing to your mother or father, who lives some distance away. The telephones are all out of order, so the only way to tell them what has happened is to write a letter.

1. Look at the pictures and at the writing you have done so far. Think about how the Willcoxes must have *felt* while all this was going on.
2. Write a short paragraph about what happened in pictures A–C.
3. Write a second paragraph about pictures D–F.
4. Write a third paragraph describing how the story ended.

Exercise C

The Willcoxes have been told that because their home has been damaged, they may receive some money to help them out. They have to write to the Council explaining what happened and what was damaged. Imagine that you are Alan or Gemma. Write two paragraphs: the first explains what happened; the second says what damage was caused.

Summing up what you've learned

How?

Ways of writing

There are four main ways of writing:

- **story** – telling a story
- **description** – telling the reader about the appearance of something
- **explanation** – telling the reader how something works
- **argument** – expressing an opinion or point of view.

How language changes

We can usually tell when something was written a long time ago from:

- **vocabulary** – some words are no longer used or have changed their meanings
- **grammar** – the way in which we construct sentences is different today from what it was in the past.

Main verbs and auxiliary verbs

If the verb in a sentence is just one word, then it is a **main verb.** Here the verb is underlined:

Cold air sinks.
The tree fell down.

If the sentence verb is more than one word, then it will contain a main verb and one or more **auxiliary verbs**:

The tree	*has*	*fallen*	*down*
	AUXILIARY VERB	MAIN VERB	

Main verbs are usually verbs that you can look up in the dictionary and find a meaning for.

Common auxiliary verbs are:
am/is/are/was/were
has been/have been/had been
has/have/had
shall/should/will/would
can/could/may/might
must/ought

Forms of the verb

Verbs can be used in five different forms. Many verbs are regular, like *walk*. A number of common verbs are irregular, like *go* and *hurt*.

Present tense	Past tense	Present participle	Past participle	Infinitive
fall(s)	fell	falling	fallen	to fall
walk(s)	walked	walking	walked	to walk
am/is/are	was/were	being	been	to be

Teenage life

Yuri is making a programme about teenage life in this country. He has started by interviewing a group of 'typical teenagers'.

- Do you think there is such a thing as a 'typical teenager'? If so, how would you describe one?
- What sort of questions do you think Yuri should ask the teenagers he interviews?

In this unit you will learn about:

Writing about memories of your early life

Differences between spoken and written English

Different past tenses and when we use them

Simplifying difficult stories

Writing good lead sentences for your paragraphs

Teenage autobiographies

The two extracts on this page are by well-known writers. Each extract comes from the beginning of the writer's memories of being a teenager.

Exercise A

1. In the extract that follows, there are two paragraphs. Write one short sentence for each one, summing up what it is about.
2. The writer uses only one tense in this extract. Which tense? Is this the tense you would expect in a piece of writing like this?

He's sixteen and a half. He is about six feet tall, fair-haired, ginger jacketed, grey-trousered, pink faced. He parts his hair right over on one side, which gives him a schoolboyish look. He bites his nails but will soon give up that schoolboy habit. For Nick, school is over! He's free! He's his real self at last!

Where is he? On the pavement of a middle-class London suburb. There are big, solid, Victorian houses on either side of the road. The front doors have stained-glass picture panes, solid brass door knockers, glossy coats of dark paint.

Exercise B

3. In the extract that follows, there are two paragraphs. Write one short sentence for each one, summing up what it is about.
4. What tenses does the writer use? Are they the tenses you would expect in a piece of writing like this?

The gibbons woke me with the dawn. Their whooping cries would draw me out of dreams, teasing and cajoling, like a parent gently waking a sleeping child. I usually woke on my back, staring at the Perspex skylight roof of the caravan. To me, the gibbons chased away the night and welcomed the day. I did not live in the jungle, I lived in the zoo.

My parents' caravan was sited, with other caravans, in a corner of Belle Vue Zoo, Manchester, near the gibbons' cage. The cage housed an entire colony of gibbons. It was an enormous square meshed palace of trees and truck-tyre swings.

Exercise C

5. Each writer has chosen a different starting point for his memories. Describe each starting point in one sentence.
6. The writers use different tenses for their memories. One is more unusual than the other. Which one is it and what effect does it have as you read it?
7. There is something else unusual about one of the two memories. Can you see what it is?
8. Which of the two extracts makes you more interested in reading the rest of the writer's memories and why?

Spoken and written memories

The writer John Gordon was interviewed about how he first became interested in writing. He also *wrote* an autobiography of his own teenage years.

Exercise A

Part of the text that follows comes from the interview; part of it comes from the written autobiography. Read the whole text and then answer the questions at the end.

1 When I was at school I was told to do an essay on snow … a composition on snow … for … a … homework and it was the middle of summer and I didn't want to do it anyway so I … so I sat on my bedroom floorboards and said I'll get rid of this old stuff and I wrote things like … er … the snow lay like a blanket all over the ground and then for some reason it occurred to me well … er … yeh … I like snow I always did like snow and … er … snow does in fact look like a blanket but most blankets I know are warm and snow is cold.

2 So I abandoned that and put down that the snow was like a sheet, which was at least white and cold. It was still not right, but now I was beginning to feel the cold of the snow and could hear my feet crunch in it. But crunch was simply the normal word and it had lost its power. I listened again as my foot broke through the crust and felt it being compacted under the sole of my boot. As the snow was pressed down, the crunch was accompanied by a squeak, and suddenly I saw that I could combine both sounds in one word. I wrote: 'the snow creaked underfoot'.

3 It sounded a lot better than your feet crunched in the snow because creaked has a lot of little echoes it's like wind in cold houses and things like that so it's a colder word and it worked better … and four hours later I was still doing my homework and I'd loved every minute of it.

1. Which parts are written and which parts are spoken?
2. Give as many reasons as you can to explain how you know which parts are spoken. For each reason quote from the text to back up what you are saying.
3. Choose a part that is spoken. Write it out in correct written sentences. Make sure that you get the punctuation right.

I have seen them, didn't I?

As you can see, Yuri gets his tenses mixed up when he talks about the past. What should he have said? And why is what he did say wrong?

Exercise A

In each of these sentences Yuri has got the tenses of the verb wrong. For each one:

a write out the verbs he has used
b write what he should have said.

1. Yesterday I was meeting a group of teenagers.
2. I have interviewed six of them yesterday afternoon.
3. Today I arrange to meet some more.
4. The teenagers I have interviewed yesterday are telling me a lot of interesting things.
5. One has told me about popular music.
6. Another is saying that she is a football fan and is supporting Glasgow Rangers.
7. I never visited Glasgow myself.
8. When I used to be a child I am playing football.

Explaining past tenses

Exercise A

In each of these sentences there is a verb in brackets, sometimes with another word, like 'not'. For each one write the correct form of the verb(s) and if there is another word, like 'not', put it in the right place.

1. Her family (live) in Brockworth since 1995.
2. Henry VIII (be) King of England.
3. Sheila phoned yesterday, but she (not phone) today.
4. Paris (be) the capital of France for centuries.
5. England and Scotland (be) separate countries until the beginning of the seventeenth century.
6. I can't tell you whether I like *Macbeth*; I (never see) it.
7. Matthew (not do) his homework yesterday.
8. Sarah (not do) her homework yet.
9. The train (already leave).
10. The train (leave) five minutes early.

Exercise B

In Exercise A above you used two tenses:

- the simple past tense: ***She gave me the book yesterday.***
- the present perfect tense: ***I have lived here since the beginning of March.***

Yuri needs help in understanding the difference between these two.

1. Write an explanation of how the present perfect is formed.
2. Write an explanation of when we use it rather than the simple past. Give examples from the sentences in Exercise A above.

Exercise C

English has several different ways of talking about the past.

Last week Yuri finished his programme about the floods. When he had completed it, he started planning his next programme. He was working on it when I interviewed him.

There are three tenses here:

- ***Yuri finished his programme.*** (simple past)
- ***He was working on it.*** (past continuous)
- ***He had completed it.*** (past perfect)

Can you work out when we use each of these three tenses? Write three or four sentences explaining how and why we use them.

Rescues

Exercise A

In this extract the verbs are in brackets, followed by a number. Write down the number of each verb and then the correct form of the verb.

I ___1 (save)___ a little girl from drowning, but that was in Wisbech where the canal from Upwell ran through the town. It was a stagnant waterway, unused except for skating in winter, and one summer day I ___2 (walk)___ home from school along its bank when a shriek ___3 (go)___ up. A woman ___4 (crouch)___ at the water's edge on the opposite side and frantically reaching out to a spot where her daughter ___5 (disappear)___.

Only the girl's hair ___6 (show)___, spread out on the water beyond her mother's fingertips. I ___7 (drop)___ my books, threw off my jacket on the way down the bank and dived. I had the girl out in seconds, and her mother ___8 (take)___ me into their house on the canal side to dry off. She loaned me a pair of her husband's trousers to give me something dry and later, when the news ___9 (get)___ into the paper, she called at our house and forced a ten-shilling note on my mother, which I ___10 (try)___ to return but it all got too embarrassing so I kept it.

Exercise B

In this part of the story, the verbs have been cut out. They are listed below. Write the number of each blank and the correct form of the verb that should fill it.

Verbs

be	*fall*
get	*hear*
mean	*meet*
realise	*pump*
see	*try*

There ___11___ more danger from germs than drowning for either the girl or me, but on two other occasions the water almost ___12___ a victim while I was nearby. Wisbech swimming pool was on the river bank below the town and it was filled from the Nene, which ___13___ that it looked like a vat of cocoa. I hauled a boy out of that when nobody else ___14___ that he was lying on the bottom and almost dead, and ever afterwards his mother mentioned it whenever she ___15___ mine.

The other occasion was more serious. A young boy ___16___ into the river itself. The grass bank was almost vertical at the spot where he'd gone in and he ___17___ to hold on to the piling but couldn't get a grip because of the slime. The current was on the verge of tugging him away when I ___18___ his brother's shout. Once again I ___19___ hair floating on the water but, with someone hanging on to my hand, I got a grip on him. A man hauled him up and ___20___ him out.

Gainful employment

Exercise A

Yuri has been trying to understand the following story about a teenager who has just left school. He finds it very difficult. Read it carefully and then follow the instructions at the end.

Nick's mother says, 'I have arranged for you to see Gareth and Judy. At their flat, next Tuesday, six-thirty. They may be able to help get you a job.'

On Tuesday Nick takes the tube to another London suburb (his mother had to give him the fare) and rings the bell of Gareth and Judy's flat. He takes the modern lift with modern strip lighting and modern buttons to press. It is all very unlike home.

Standing outside the door of No. 11, he hears the clitter-clatter of two typewriters. As usual, Judy and Gareth are hard at work. The sound both excites and frightens Nick. It is exciting because these are real grown-ups, real writers working for money. It is frightening because he wants to be like them. But will he ever be?

He rings the bell. Judy opens the door. 'Oh, Nick, of course, is it six-thirty already? Come in, we're both in a mess, I've got to finish a thing for tomorrow and Gareth's got a broadcast, but lovely to see you, come in!'

She is short, plump and not pretty but something better than pretty. She moves quickly, like a bird. Gareth, also short and plump, takes his time about everything, deliberately and amusingly. They set each other off to perfection. Judy works on a portable Corona, Gareth on a portable Underwood. Both machines are surrounded by typing, his neatly stacked and hers in a mess all over the big table. Professionals.

Yuri finds this difficult for two reasons:

- It is about the past, but it is written in the present tense ('Nick's mother **says** …', not 'Nick's mother **said** ….')
- It is written by Nick about Nick, but he calls himself 'he'. ('**Nick's** mother says …', not '**My** mother says ….')

It would be easier for Yuri to understand if it said, 'My mother said …', rather than 'Nick's mother says ….'

Choose a section of about ten lines and rewrite it so that Yuri will understand it more clearly.

Writing a memory

On page 68 we looked at the beginnings of two short autobiographies: memories of growing up. Now you are going to write the beginning of your autobiography.

Exercise A

Begin by making a chart of your life so far. Your chart should look like the one below. Fill in all the information you can. Start with 'now' and work backwards.

Year	Home	School	Important events in my life	Other important events I remember
1999	Baby Gemma born	Moved to Willingdon High School	Broke my ankle	
1998	Moved to Lodder		Won cup in swimming sports	Man United won Premier League
1997				
1996				
1995				

Exercise B

Now you need to decide how to start your autobiography.

- Look back to page 68 and see how the two writers there started their autobiographies.
- Now read the extract on the opposite page, which is how John Gordon began his.

None of these writers begins at the beginning. Each chooses a **key moment** and describes it vividly. Then they go on to explain how they came to be in that situation.

1. Look at the chart you made in Exercise A. Use it to jog your memory. Try to find an event in your life that was important, or vivid, or exciting, or funny, or a combination of these.
2. Jot down all you can remember about that memory. Don't worry about writing complete sentences. Try to 'see' the memory in your mind and write down the details of what you can see.

Exercise C

Now write the first draft of two paragraphs describing your memory. Remember that each paragraph should have:

- a lead sentence that introduces it
- three or four sentences that describe what happened
- a concluding sentence that rounds it off.

The night was so black that although I could hear the tide slur along the ship's side I could not see the water a few feet below. We were well offshore, tied up to a buoy in midstream, and only the occasional glint of a hooded headlight showed where Harwich lay in the blackness. There had been no air raids anywhere along the coast, no flash of bomb or gun, not even an angling search light to distract the man on watch.

I was bored. My mate Molyneux had gone below where they were brewing a new can of tea on the messdeck, and I was on watch alone. I went to the ship's side and leant on the rail ... but someone had removed a section, and I leant into empty air.

Exercise D

Look at what you have written. Look particularly at your lead sentences.

Paragraph 1

The lead sentence of your first paragraph is very important. It should catch the reader's attention. Look at these lead sentences:

The gibbons woke me with the dawn.

The night was so black that although I could hear the tide slur along the ship's side I could not see the water a few feet below.

Each of them sets the scene in a few words and makes it sound interesting and unusual. Try to do the same with your first sentence

Paragraph 2

The lead sentence of this paragraph should make a link with the first paragraph. Look at the examples on page 68 and this page to see how those writers did this. Try to do the same with your second paragraph.

Exercise E

Changing the two lead sentences probably means that you need to make some changes to the other sentences in your first draft. Make a second draft including any other changes you need to make.

Summing up what you've learned

Spoken and written English

When we speak we often make things up as we go along. This makes spoken English different from written English. These are some of the differences:

- We repeat ourselves.
- We hesitate and put in words like 'um' and 'er'.
- We change track in the middle of a sentence.
- Our sentences run together and use a lot of connecting words like 'and' and 'then'.

This doesn't mean that our sentences are 'bad' or 'ungrammatical'. It is a natural result of the way in which conversations happen.

Different kinds of tense

We have already seen that each tense comes in two versions:

	Simple	**Continuous**
Present	she walks	she is walking
Past	she walked	she was walking

There is also a third version of each tense:

	Perfect
Present	she has walked
Past	she had walked

Describing things that happened in the past

Present perfect

We use the present perfect to describe something that happened (or started) in the past, but which is still important in the present. So if I say, ***Her family has lived in Brockworth since 1996***, they are still living in Brockworth now.

Simple past

The simple past is used to describe a completed action in the past; for example: ***I met her yesterday***.

Past continuous

This is used to describe an action which was still going on when something else happens: ***As they were driving to Brighton they saw an accident***.

Past perfect

The past perfect is used to describe an action which happened before another action in the past: ***After they had left the classroom they walked to the library***.

UNIT 8

Future Theme Park

Most theme parks are about the past or the present. This one will be devoted to the future.

- How would you explain to Yuri what a theme park is?
- Do you think a future theme park would attract a lot of visitors?
- What kind of thing would it contain?

In this unit you will learn about:

The vocabulary of the future

How words are made

Using verbs to describe the future

Writing from notes

Writing your own predictions up to the year 2025

What is 'robot'?

Yuri would like some help in understanding words connected with the future. He's too lazy to use a dictionary so he keeps on asking Sarah-Jane – who has other work to do.

Exercise A

This is the first list of words that Yuri has asked about:

clone ***database*** ***robot*** ***software***

For each word:

1. Write an explanation of what it means.
2. Make up a sentence that uses it correctly and shows its meaning.

Example

Word: ***videophone***

Definition: ***A videophone is a telephone which makes it possible for the speakers to see each other as well as hear each other.***

Sentence: ***I spoke to Jennie on the videophone yesterday but she wasn't looking at all well.***

Exercise B

Now do the same for these words and phrases:

global warming ***recycling*** ***satellite dish*** ***solar energy***
biodegradable ***DNA*** ***edutainment*** ***virtual reality***

... and 'nanorobot'?

The chances are that you don't know what a *nanorobot* is. A robot, yes, but 'nano-'? Something to do with grandmothers? Try using this information to help you work it out.

1. The Latin word 'nanus' means 'dwarf'.
2. A 'nanosecond' is 1/1000,000,000 of a second.

So what do you think a nanorobot is?

Prefix and stem

Some words like ***nanorobot*** begin with a **prefix**. This is a group of letters **fix**ed **pre** (before) the main part of the word. The main part of the word is called the **stem**. So the word ***nanorobot*** has two parts:

nano	***robot***
↑	↑
PREFIX	STEM

Exercise A

Divide each of these words into prefix and stem:

hypermarket ***microsurgery*** ***prefix*** ***superhuman***

Exercise B

Use your knowledge about language to work out the answers to these questions:

1. **a** What is the difference between a ***supermarket*** and a ***hypermarket***?
   b So what do you think the difference is between ***supersonic speed*** and ***hypersonic speed***?
2. A ***megaton*** is a million tons. A ***megaphone*** makes your voice sound very, very loud. The Greek word ***lithos*** means a stone. So what is a ***megalith***?
3. What do you think a ***super-rat*** might be?

Talking about the future

Yuri doesn't understand the different ways in which we talk about the future.

Exercise A

There are three sentences on the page Yuri is reading. Each contains a verb. For each sentence:

1. Write down the whole verb.
2. The sentences show three different ways in which we can talk about the future. Explain to Yuri in writing how each one works.

Exercise B

In each of these sentences the verb is in brackets. Write out the correct future form of the verb.

1. Tomorrow my father __(take)__ us to the seaside.
2. Do you think it __(rain)__ this afternoon?
3. Our class __(go)__ to the theatre on Friday week.
4. It __(be)__ my birthday next Tuesday.
5. If Emma comes this evening, we __(do)__ our homework together.
6. After school finishes today, Peter and I __(play)__ basketball.

Exercise C

We often use time words or phrases to show that we are talking about the future. For example:

tomorrow ***next week***

1. Write down the time words and phrases used in the sentences in Exercise B.
2. Each of the time words or phrases below refers to the past. Write the corresponding one for the future.

Example:

yesterday → ***tomorrow***

last year →
two weeks ago →
the day before yesterday →

The future? I'm not sure ...

1 The Theme Park <u>will</u> open next year.
2 The Theme Park <u>may</u> open next year.
3 The Theme Park <u>might</u> open next year.
4 The Theme Park <u>can</u> open next year.
5 The Theme Park <u>could</u> open next year.
6 The Theme Park <u>must</u> open next year.

Exercise A

What's the difference? English has so many different ways of talking about the future, it is sometimes difficult to know which one to choose. It is certainly hard to explain to people like Yuri.

1. Look at sentences 1 and 2. Imagine that they are part of a conversation between two people who don't agree. One thinks that the theme part *will* open next year. The other one only thinks it *may* open next year:

   ***A:** Look at the mess the builders have made. They're never going to open on time.*
   ***B:** Oh yes, the Theme Park will open next year.*
   ***A:** I doubt it. Of course the Theme Park <u>may</u> open next year, but I'm not holding my breath.*

   Explain to Yuri what the difference is between the two sentences.

2. Now compare sentences 2 and 6. Write a short conversation like the example above. Then explain the difference between the two sentences.

3. Now do the same for sentences 4 and 5.

Life in the future

Exercise A

In this paragraph some of the verbs have been missed out. They are listed in the wrong order below. Write the number of each blank and the correct form of the verb that should fill it.

Verbs

be *cause* *have*
kill *provide* *share*

Environment friendly

Technological progress ___1___ us with many advantages, and will continue to do so in the future. But there ___2___ a price to pay – the damaged ozone layer and the effects of greenhouse gases ___3___ terrible consequences for the future of our planet. Air pollution ___4___ acid rain, and water contamination ___5___ wildlife. Some natural resources are rapidly being used up, and many large tracts of rainforest have been destroyed. Because of our actions, some of the animals we ___6___ the planet with are extinct, while others are endangered. If we do not take a more responsible attitude towards our finite resources, the results will be catastrophic.

Exercise B

In this paragraph some of the verbs have been missed out. No help is given. Work out a suitable verb for each space and write it in the correct form.

Easy living

Imagine standing at a bus stop when suddenly your 'hot badge' ___7___ that the person behind you ___8___ the same music. This might be all you need to know to start a conversation and ___9___ friends. Our everyday lives may soon be changed forever because of clever inventions like this one. Emotion containers will be filled with precious gifts, while an intelligent garbage can [dustbin] ___10___ out domestic rubbish. Friendly robots ___11___ how to perform simple tasks and ___12___ unique personalities. Some jobs, such as shopping or going to the bank, can already be done from home on the Internet, and soon we will be able to consult a doctor in the same way. Travel will be made more fun with electronic travel guides and 'ear-ins' that translate foreign languages.

Virtual reality

On this page there are two texts about virtual reality. The text in Exercise A describes what it is. Exercise B looks at the future of virtual reality.

Exercise A

A number of words are missing from this extract. Read it carefully and try to work out what should go in each space. Write the number of the space and the word you have chosen.

The five senses are ___1___, sound, touch, smell and ___2___. They give us ___3___ about the real world: about the shape of objects, their position, colour, texture, temperature and chemical make-up.

Imagine a ___4___ which sends information to your senses – but not information about the ___5___ world around you. It sends pretend information, information about an ___6___ world. Your senses are fooled into thinking this imaginary world is real. It isn't, but you ___7___ it is. It is virtually real.

A virtual world is a world created by a computer. It looks real and ___8___ real, even though it is not real. And ___9___ it isn't real, some of the things in it might not be ___10___ in the real world.

Exercise B

Here the text has been cut right down. All you have left is the skeleton. Use this skeleton to write three paragraphs of your own. **Remember that this text is all about the *future*.**

Paragraph 1

- virtual reality in a few years' time?
- impossible to predict accurately
- certainly used more and more

Paragraph 2

virtual reality:

- makes learning more fun/easier
- experience things only read about before (live in medieval village, fly down volcano, design + drive own car)
- jargon word: 'edutainment'

Paragraph 3

enthusiasts think:

- virtual reality – ultimate way escape from real world
- (better than best computer game ever!)
- enter virtual worlds –
- example: explore world at time of dinosaurs – recreated (virtual Jurassic Park) – enter world – watch pterodactyls – wander through Jurassic swamps – become tasty snack for Tyrannosaurus rex

Looking into the future

Now it's your chance to peer into the future. On this page are some experts' predictions of what may happen in the years up to 2025. Read them through. Then follow the instructions in Exercises A and B.

2005 Various forms of electronic addiction become a problem
2007 Video watch
2009 Fire-fighting robots that can find and rescue people
2011 Housework robots to fetch, carry, clean, tidy and organize
2014 Nanorobots roaming in blood vessels under own power
2014 Robotic pets
2014 First human landing on Mars
2020 Artificial lungs, kidneys and brain cells
2020 Cars that drive themselves on smart highways
2025 Deep underground cities in Japan
2025 Extension of lifespan to over 100
2030 More robots than people in developed countries

These events are predicted and could happen at any time. But when?

- Collapse of the world's fisheries
- Asteroid hits Earth
- Viruses become immune to all known treatments
- Collapse of the United Nations
- First unambiguous (definite) contact with extraterrestrial life
- Worldwide epidemic
- Time travel invented

Exercise A

Getting your ideas together

1. Read through the timetable on the left.
2. Make a list of three or four ideas there that you think will be good for human beings, and that you would find interesting to write about.
3. Add as many ideas of your own as you can.

Planning

4. Make a plan for one paragraph explaining why life in the future will be good. Choose 2–4 points from your 'good' list.

Drafting

5. Now write a first draft of paragraph 1. Leave two lines before you write your first sentence. Write 4–6 sentences and include as many of your list of points as you can.
6. Look at what you have written. Think of a good sentence to lead in to what you have written (your **lead sentence**). Write it in the space you left at the beginning.

Exercise A *(continued)*

7. Think of a good sentence to round off what you have written. Write it at the end.

Revising

8. Read through your paragraph. Answer these questions and change your paragraph if you think you need to:
   - Does the first sentence make people want to read the rest of the paragraph?
   - Does the first sentence lead naturally into the second?
   - Is the main part of the paragraph (the **body**) clear and easy to understand?
   - Does the last sentence (the **conclusion**) sum the paragraph up neatly and clearly?

Exercise B

You are going to add two more paragraphs about 'Life in the future':

- **Paragraph 2:** How life might become worse.
- **Paragraph 3:** Your feelings about life in the future.

Thinking

9. Read through the timetable on page 84.
10. Make a list of three or four ideas there that you think will be bad for human beings, and that you would find interesting to write about.
11. Add as many ideas of your own as you can.

Planning

12. Make a plan for one paragraph explaining why life in the future will be bad. Choose 2–4 points from your 'bad' list.
13. Think about your own feelings about the future: do you think life will be good or bad? And what are your reasons? Make a plan for a paragraph explaining your ideas.

Drafting

14. Now draft paragraphs 2 and 3 just as you did paragraph 1 (Exercise A, nos. 5–7).

Revising

15. Revise these two paragraphs as you did paragraph 1 (Exercise A, no. 8). Try to make sure that paragraph 1 leads on to paragraph 2 and paragraph 2 leads on to paragraph 3.

Summing up what you've learned

Word structure

All words have a **stem**. Many words also have a **prefix**:

Prefix	Stem
	market
super	*market*
mega	*phone*

If you know what the prefix means, you can sometimes work out the meaning of the whole word. These are some common prefixes that tell us about size:

mini *small*
micro *very small*
super *big*
mega *very big*
hyper *very big indeed*

Future tenses

There are three common ways of using verbs to talk about the future:

will/shall

We put *will* before the verb:

She will write a letter.

Sometimes, when we use *I* or *we*, we use *shall*:

I shall tell your father.

going to

This is also a very common way of talking about the future:

She is going to write a letter.
I am going to tell your father.

the present continuous

We use the present continuous to talk about fixed arrangements:

I am taking GCSEs in June.

Other ways of talking about the future

There are other words we can use – especially if we are not so sure about what is going to happen. Some very common ones are used in these sentences and underlined:

She may write a letter.
I might tell your father.
She can write a letter.
I could tell your father.

It is sometimes difficult to know which one to choose. Usually *might* and *could* make it seem *less likely* that it will happen:

She may write a letter.
(Who knows? Maybe she will and maybe she won't.)

I might tell your father.
(I may do, but it isn't very likely.)

9

UNIT 9

Protest campaign

Yuri and the team are making a programme about a protest campaign.

- What are these people protesting about?
- What do you think are the main reasons for their campaign?
- Would you be on their side or against them, and why?
- Do you think campaigns of this sort are worthwhile?

In this unit you will learn about:

The difference between a written argument and other disagreements

The words we use to link ideas in an argument

Different kinds of sentence starting with 'if'

How to write argument sentences and paragraphs

Argument, squabble or battle?

When we disagree with other people we can express ourselves in many different ways.

Exercise A

1. Choose one of the pictures.
2. Think about what the two people might be saying to each other.
3. Write a short script of the conversation.

Exercise B

4. Think about what is going on in each of the four pictures.
5. You could say that each of the pictures showed an *argument*. Or you could use a different word. Look at the two lists of words at the top of the next page and choose one from each list to describe what is going on in the picture. Explain why you chose them.

Exercise C

You can combine words in List 1 with those in List 2 to make phrases:

heated argument
irritable quarrel

6. Make up three phrases like that.
7. For each one, explain what you think it would be like and when it might happen.

List 1

angry	calm	cool
crazy	heated	hot-headed
illogical	irritable	logical
reasonable	senseless	sensible
thoughtful	understanding	unreasonable
wild	wise	

List 2

argument	battle	controversy
debate	disagreement	discussion
dispute	fight	quarrel
row	run-in	squabble
tiff	wrangle	

Exercise D

Each of these three texts is about the same subject. Read them through and then answer the questions at the bottom of the page.

A

When my Gran comes to stay Dad turns the heating up. He says she feels the cold. I can't stand it when the living room is as hot as that. I usually go round to my friends. I bet it puts the gas bill up, too.

B

Every time we burn gas, coal, oil or logs, we send carbon dioxide into the atmosphere and make it more likely that the Greenhouse Effect will change our weather. So, unless there's an old person or a small baby in the room, burn just enough to keep warm without getting boiling hot. If your house has central heating, ask whether there is a room thermostat. There should be. This switches the system off when a certain temperature is reached. 20°C (68°F) is usually comfortable for a living room.

C

Why's this room so hot? Have you been messing around with that thermostat again? Just leave it alone – otherwise you can spend the evening in your room with no heating – and no tea!

Answer these questions for each of the three texts.

1. Who do you think said or wrote these words?
2. Who do you think they were aimed at?
3. How would you describe what is said or written? Use words from List 1 and List 2 in your answer.

Argument words

Yuri is finding some of the 'little words' in English very trying. See if you can help him out by explaining when we use them.

Exercise A

Sarah-Jane has collected some sentences for Yuri showing how we use some of the words he finds difficult. Read them through and then answer the questions that follow.

We can't go to the film <u>because</u> we haven't got any money.
<u>As</u> it's raining the cricket match has been cancelled.
Dave was ill, <u>so</u> he didn't go to school.
He worked hard <u>but</u> he still failed the test.

1. Look carefully at the first sentence. Write an explanation of when we use the word ***because***.
2. Write a sample sentence of your own using ***because***.
3. Now do the same for ***as***, ***so*** and ***but***.
4. Yuri is also puzzled by ***since*** and ***therefore***. Write an explanation of each of these and make up a sample sentence for each one.

Exercise B

Sometimes we can use a group of words, a phrase, instead of the single words we've been looking at:

<u>and as a result</u>
Dave was ill, ~~so~~ he didn't go to school.

Here are some other phrases we can use in a similar way:

- ***for this reason***
- ***so that***
- ***with the result that***

1. Which of the 'little words' from Exercise A can replace each of these phrases?
2. For each of the phrases make up one or two sentences showing how it is used. For example: ***When I got home I felt very tired. <u>For this reason</u> I couldn't finish my homework.***

If ...

Another word Yuri has problems with is ***if***. English people seem to use it in so many different ways ...

If global warming heated up the oceans it would affect tiny sea plants called plankton. If plankton were destroyed in the Antarctic, the lives of the whales that feed on them would also be threatened.

Exercise A

We can make different kinds of 'if' sentence: some are about the future, and some are about the past. Is each of these sentences about the future or the past?

1. If it is fine tomorrow we'll go fishing.
2. If Gina had done her homework last night, Mrs Thomas would not have been so angry with her.
3. If I get my homework done early, I'll watch a film on TV.
4. If you had told the truth we wouldn't be in such a mess.
5. If everyone told the truth all the time, life would be very embarrassing.
6. If you were my friend, you would give me some of that chocolate.

Exercise B

When we make 'if' sentences about the future, we can show our feelings about the subject. We can show we think it could very well happen and is 'possible':

> ***If Granny gives me money for my birthday I will buy some CDs.***

Or we can show we think it is possible, but we aren't at all sure it will happen:

> ***If I won the Lottery jackpot I would buy a Rolls-Royce.***

Is each of these sentences 'possible' or 'not at all sure'?

1. If Claire wins the 100 metres, she will be picked for the school team.
2. If you came over to my house, I would mend your bike.
3. If you don't put that thing away, I'm going to take it away from you.
4. If global warming heated up the oceans it would affect tiny sea plants called plankton.

Ifs and buts

Exercise A

In this text some words have been missed out. They are listed below, together with other words that do not belong in the text. Write the number of each blank and the word you think should go in it.

Words

also	*although*
and	*but*
if	*really*
unless	*when*

Factory farming

Factory farming – keeping a great many birds or animals together in one place, usually in confined spaces and without access to daylight – enables farmers to grow more food ___1___ to sell it more cheaply ___2___ it also causes a number of problems. ___3___ one animal or bird has a disease it is passed on very quickly to the others and this encourages the spread of the viruses and bacteria that cause such diseases as salmonella. ___4___, hundreds of animals in one place produce an enormous amount of dung. Mixed with urine, this is called slurry. Some is used as fertiliser on fields and some is just washed away. Slurry is very strong and ___5___ it finds its way into rivers it causes serious pollution.

Exercise B

In this text some words have been missed out. Write the number of each blank and the word you think should go in it.

Organic farming

___6___, a growing number of farmers, concerned about the effects of chemicals on the environment and on our food, have turned to organic methods. They use natural compost and animal manure to fertilise their fields. They use 'crop rotation' instead of growing the same thing on the same field every year. ___7___ they don't wear out the soil or let the numbers of pests which attack a particular crop build up. They don't use chemical sprays, ___8___ instead increase the 'natural resistance' of their crops and animals to pests, diseases and so on. Naturally, there are drawbacks. It takes at least two years before the land can be 'cured' of all the chemicals that had been poured on to it in the past. For those years, a farmer switching to organic farming may earn very little. ___9___, organic farming means more hand labour for the farmer – or more workers to employ and pay – ___10___ the food is more expensive to produce. Partly for these reasons, organic farmers are still hugely outnumbered by the rest.

Building argument sentences

When you are writing an argument, you often need to write sentences that:

- provide information
- explain why it is important.

For example:

INFORMATION	SENTENCE
Cars in England: 2,000,000 new cars every year – 1,500,000 old cars scrapped – 500,000 more cars on road per year	In England there are two million new cars every year **but** only one and a half million old cars are scrapped, **so** the number of cars on the road goes up by half a million every year.

Notice how the facts are connected by 'little words' like ***but*** and ***so***.

Exercise A

Write sentences using all this information. Write as few sentences as possible.

More cars:
- more metal used
- more energy needed in factories
- more scrap heaps (ugly, wasteful)

Exercise B

Write sentences using the information in this table. Write as few sentences as possible.

Pollution produced by cars with petrol engines

Polluting chemical	Effects
Nitrogen oxide	Acid rain
Carbon monoxide	Poisonous to human beings
Carbon dioxide	Main 'greenhouse' gas

Writing an argument

One of the protest groups that Yuri has interviewed is campaigning against using cars too much. They are preparing a leaflet for children aged 8–10, explaining why we should all use cars less. This page contains information about the problems caused by the increasing numbers of cars on the road. They want to use this in the leaflet. Read the information and then do the exercises on page 95.

A

- 1989 record traffic jam: 130km (80 mile) long
- 1 km motorway takes 6.5 hectares of land
- 1980-89: 430km (270 miles) of motorway built in Britain – covering 28 square kilometres (11 square miles)

B People killed or injured in traffic accidents during 1988

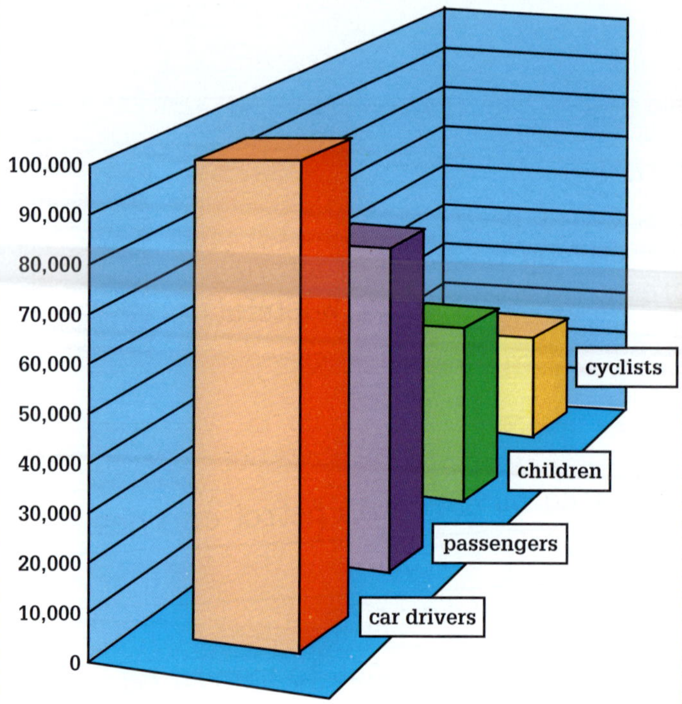

C Fuel consumption per year in Britain for road transport
petrol: 30 billion litres (6.8 billion gallons)
diesel: 11 billion litres (2.4 billion gallons)

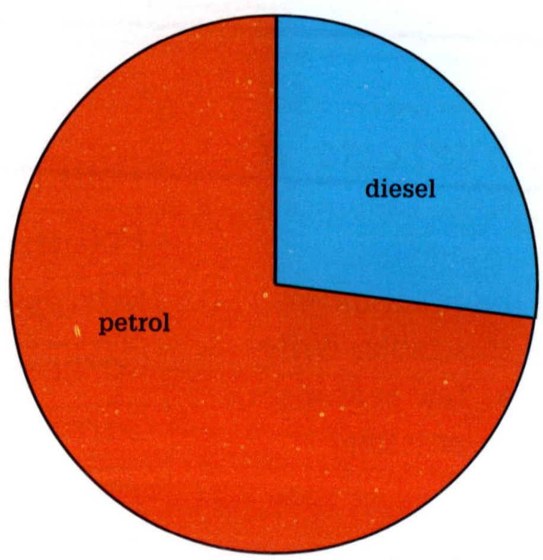

You are going to prepare the leaflet. It will be a single sheet of A4, folded – as in the diagram on the right. It will have four pages. Each of the exercises below explains how to write one of the pages.

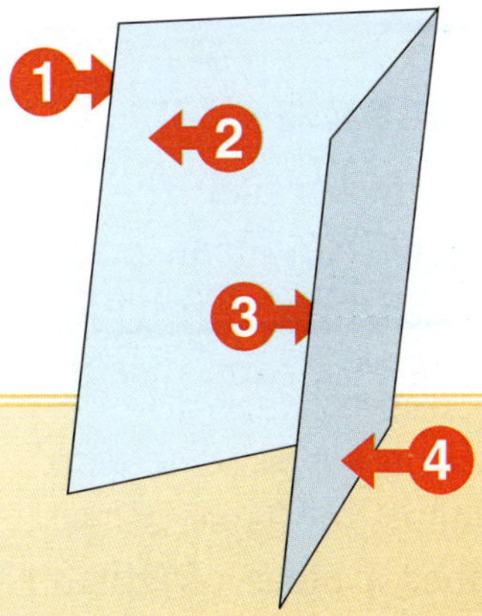

Exercise A – Page 1

1. Look at the information in Block A on page 94.
2. There are four pieces of information there:
   - about a traffic jam
   - about how much land one kilometre of motorway uses up
   - about how many kilometres of motorway were built in the 1980s
   - about how much land this used up altogether.
3. Write one sentence for each of these four pieces of information.
4. Think of one or two pictures to illustrate the sentences you have written. Write a short description of each one.

Exercise B – Page 2

5. Now do the same thing for the information in Blocks B and C on page 94. Write 2–5 sentences for each and describe one or two illustrations for each.

Exercise C – Page 3

6. Now look back to page 93. This contains a lot of information about how cars add to pollution. Use this information to write 3–5 sentences.
7. Describe one or two pictures that can be used to illustrate these sentences.

Exercise D – Page 4

8. On the back page of the leaflet you are going to tell your readers how they can help by using cars less. Think about ways in which people can avoid using cars unnecessarily. Write 3–5 sentences explaining this.
9. Describe one or two pictures that can be used to illustrate these sentences.

Summing up what you've learned

Arguments

In everyday speech the word 'argument' can mean many different things – from an angry squabble to a calm discussion.

In writing we use the word 'argument' in a special way. It describes a piece of writing that:

- puts across a point of view
- gives reasons for the point of view
- has a beginning, a middle and an end.

An example of this kind of argument is text B on page 89.

Argument words

When you write an argument you need words that link the parts of your argument together. They help you show that one part leads on to the next. Some of the commonest of these words are:

as	***because***	***but***
since	***so***	***therefore***

You can also use short phrases that have similar meanings. For example:

as a result
for this reason
so that
with the result that

Using 'if'

We make sentences starting with 'if' to talk about possibilities:

If you don't stop talking …
If only I had looked more carefully …

'If' sentences can be:

- about the future (***If you don't stop talking …***)
- about the past (***If only I had looked more carefully …***).

We can make it clear if we think something in the future is possible or unlikely:

Possible: ***If it rains we shall get wet.***
Unlikely: ***If I won the lottery, I'd buy you a car.***

We do this by putting the verbs into a different tense.

UNIT 10

Looking back

This unit reviews some of the language points you have been looking at in Units 6–9.

In this unit you will revise:

Different kinds of writing:

- story
- description
- explanation
- argument.

Looking at words:

- stems and prefixes
- vocabulary.

Verbs:

- parts of a verb
- past, present and future tenses.

Argument words

Paragraphing

What kind of writing?

Exercise A

1. Read the four texts A–D carefully.
2. For each one, say if it is:
   - a story
   - a description
   - an explanation
   - an argument

   and give the reasons for your answer.

A

It was in an old red brick building that dated from the 1930s. It looked like a huge house, made up from a symmetrical series of boxes, with a central hall that projected out to the front gates and a pair of double doors that nobody could mistake as anything other than the entrance. This was a feature of the thirties-style school building. (Most modern secondary schools, built during the late fifties and early sixties, were designed so that any visitors would have to search hard to find the entrance.)

B

It was a sunny Sunday morning and I was in our backyard when I heard Chamberlain's tired old voice on the wireless declaring war on 'Herr Hitler'.

'Oh, Norman,' said my mother, 'what's going to happen to the boys?'

'Don't worry, woman,' said my father, 'it'll all be over before they're old enough to go.' Which was a reasonable way to think because I wasn't yet quite fourteen. But on my way to meet the evacuees the air raid siren sounded as I cycled past the gasworks, the only target Wisbech had to offer, and the thought of bombs made me uncomfortable for the first time.

C

Could genetically-engineered food help the hungry? In places like India and Pakistan, much of the soil is too salty to grow crops. But it might be possible to put a gene from a native salt-loving plant into a food crop like wheat, so that it could be grown in salty soils. Again, it sounds like a good idea. But environmental organizations like Greenpeace have argued that poverty, not lack of food, is the reason why people are starving in the Third World. Are the claims made by genetic engineering companies just propaganda?

D

Once it is slung, a hammock is quite comfortable, and certainly better than being spread out on the deck, for a hammock mattress (made of canvas, of course) is very short and you only have one blanket. If you did have to sleep on the floor or a table you had to be the first to clear away your gear in the morning, and then you had the hazard while you were eating your breakfast of having the horny foot of a matelot (sailor) from the hammock above coming down into the butter.

Looking at words

Exercise A

1. Each of these words has two parts:
   - a prefix
   - a stem.

   Write down the prefix of each word.

   hypersensitive ***superstore*** ***microcomputer***
   megaton ***minimarket***

2. Write down a different word that begins with each of the five prefixes.

Exercise B

1. Each of the following words describes a kind of weather. For each one write a sentence that uses it correctly and makes its meaning clear.

   hurricane ***breeze*** ***gale***

2. The words in this list are about different kinds of weather. Divide them into three groups according to their meaning:

   bake ***blast*** ***blaze*** ***blow***
   burn ***cascade*** ***drench*** ***drip***
   drizzle ***dry*** ***gust*** ***howl***
   pour ***scorch*** ***whistle***

3. Put the words in each group into a league table with the weakest at the top and the strongest at the bottom.

Exercise C

The words and phrases in the following lists are all about the future. For each one write a dictionary definition explaining what you think it means.

1. ***palmtop computer*** ***virtual reality*** ***cloning***
2. ***nanorobot*** ***robotics*** ***implant***

Parts of a verb

THE LANGUAGE KIT 2

Exercise A

1. In this extract some sentences or parts of sentences are printed in **bold.** After each of these there is a number. Write down the number of each sentence or part of a sentence, and then write the verb or verbs from it.

However, some of the newly engineered agricultural products might help the environment (1). Fruit and vegetables have already been designed that are resistant to insect pests and certain types of disease, and **so one day, environmentally dangerous chemicals like pesticides may be unnecessary (2).**

One particular example is a potato (3) which has been genetically engineered to commit suicide when it is infected by a disease-causing fungus. The suicidal potato has a special bacterial gene incorporated into its genetic recipe. **This gene makes a very aggressive kind of protein (4)** which stops the production of all other proteins in the potato's cells and so eventually kills it. But the gene is only switched on when the fungus attacks. The potato dies, but **in a field of potatoes this is good news (5),** because the disease is prevented from spreading – without the need for pesticides.

2. Two of the verbs you have written down contain:
   - a main verb
   - an auxiliary verb.

   Write the numbers of the two sentences and then write down the auxiliary verb in them.

3. Write two or three sentences explaining the difference between a main verb and an auxiliary verb.

Exercise B

Copy and complete this table:

Stem	Present tense		Present participle	
	walk/walks	walked		walked
go			going	gone
be				

Looking at the past

Exercise A

In this text some of the verbs have been replaced by the verb stem and a number, like this:

She __(go) 1__ there yesterday.

Write down the number of each verb and the correct form of the verb:

1 went.

'I'm sorry,' said Mum. 'But I __(get) 1__ married whether you like it or not.'

'But Mum,' I __(start) 2__ off.

'No buts,' she cut in. 'I'm lonely at night when you and Andy __(go) 3__ to bed. And anyway, I love Ralph. He is a lovely man. I thought you __(like) 4__ him too.'

'I do,' I said. 'It's not him I don't like. It's his job. He __(bury) 5__ people in the cemetery.'

'What's that got to do with it?' she asked hotly. 'I'm not going to stop loving Ralph just because he is an undertaker. You don't judge a person by their job.'

'It's embarrassing,' I said. 'Last night he __(take) 6__ us down the street to the fish and chip shop in his funeral wagon. Do you realise that our tea was brought home in a hearse? The same car that is used to cart dead bodies around. All the kids __(laugh) 7__. One idiot laid down on the footpath with a flower in his mouth as we went by and pretended he was dead. Old Mr Manor __(take) 8__ his hat off as we go past. It's the absolute pits going around in a hearse. Why doesn't he get a normal car like other people?'

'Ralph can't afford another car at the moment,' said Mum sadly. 'Business __(be) 9__ bad lately.'

'I suppose he __(wait) 10__ for an axe maniac to move into town or perhaps things would pick up if we introduced the bubonic plague.'

Exercise B

1. Write out the correct form of the verb in each of these sentences:
   - **a** Jason __(play)__ football last night.
   - **b** So far, Jason __(play)__ football every night this week.
   - **c** Jason __(play)__ football when he hurt his leg.
2. Each of the three sentences needs a different tense. For each of the three tenses, write one or two sentences explaining when we use it.

Looking into the future

Exercise A

In this text you can find four different ways of changing the form of the verb to talk about the future. Write down the four sentences and underline the verb.

'What are you doing tonight?' asked Sheena.

'Maria and I are going to see the new film at the Leisure Centre,' said Alex.

'People say it's not very good.'

'Well, if it isn't we won't stay. I want an early night. We leave for Southampton at half past six tomorrow morning.'

Exercise B

In Exercise A you found four ways of changing the verb to talk about the future. Copy and complete this table:

The future

	Verb form	Sample sentence
1	will travel	
2		She is going to travel to London this evening.
3		
4		

Exercise C

In each of these sentences one or two words are missing. The missing verbs are listed on the right. Choose the correct verb for each sentence. You can only use each word once.

Verbs
can
could
must
will
would

1. If I saw her, I _____ certainly tell her what I thought of her.
2. I _____ get there on time, but I don't think I _____.
3. You really _____ learn to look after yourself properly.
4. You look as if you are lost. _____ I help you?

Argument words

Exercise A

Yuri is still having difficulty using the little words that link parts of an argument – words like ***because*** and ***so***. On the right is something he wrote recently.

1. Find each mistake.
2. Write the number of the line it is on.
3. Write the word which is wrong.
4. Write the word he should have used.

We had a problem while we were filming yesterday because fortunately it wasn't serious. We were making a programme about traffic problems in British cities, but I wanted to film a traffic jam. So the road was very wide I decided to put the camera on a traffic island in the middle of the road. Unfortunately the camera tripod was wider than the island and because stuck out into the road a bit. We had just started filming when a large car hit the tripod and knocked it onto another car. The driver was angry - but therefore no real damage was done I told him to calm down. This just made him angrier. So he was standing in the middle of the road he made the traffic jam worse, but all the other drivers started getting angry too. In the end Sarah-Jane calmed them all down.

Exercise B

Yuri needs more help with 'if' sentences. The only way he will understand is if someone explains to him what these sentences mean. Read the sample sentences and answer Yuri's questions.

Sentences	Questions
1 ***If it had rained yesterday, we should have got wet.***	**1** Did it rain?
2 ***If Peter was at the match yesterday, I didn't see him.***	**2** Does the speaker know if Peter was at the match?
3 ***If ice is heated it melts.***	**3** When does this happen?
4 ***My dad says if I get full marks in the test I can have some extra pocket money.***	**4** When does this happen?
5 ***If I were you I'd give up smoking.***	**5** When does this happen?

Looking at paragraphs

Exercise A

These are the sentences from one paragraph of a story. It is a continuation of the story on page 101. The sentences are in the wrong order. Work out the order they should be in. Write down the letters of the sentences in that order.

A In the hearse of course.
B We all went off to the snowfields together on our honeymoon.
C Well, Mum and Ralph got married and my little brother Andy and I had a new stepfather.
D I tried everything I could think of to talk Ralph out of taking the hearse but it was no use.
E 'We can put the skis in the back and there's plenty of room for the luggage.'
F 'It's just right for the snow,' he said.

Exercise B

This is how the next two paragraphs continue the story. Again the sentences are jumbled.

1. Work out the correct order for the sentences.
2. Work out where the break between the paragraphs comes.

G A man came over and said that he knew that beef was expensive at the moment but wasn't this going a bit far?
H A real shamejob.
I We were the laughing stock of the ski slopes.
J Every day we arrived at the bottom of the ski slopes in the grey hearse with: 'R. Henderson Budget Funerals and Pet Interments' written on the door.
K Ralph would cook chops and steak.
L People called us 'The Skiing Cannibals'.
M At lunch time we would get out our portable barbecue and set it up behind the wagon.
N People came rushing over to see who had been killed.
O It was terrible.

UNIT 11

Yuri at the fashion show

Every year millions of pounds are spent on fashionable clothes. Every month dozens of different magazines come out describing the latest fashions.

- What do we mean by 'fashion'?
- Why do some people spend so much money on the latest fashions?
- What do you think is fashionable for people of your age?
- Are you interested in fashion?

In this unit you will learn about:

Words for fashion:

- garments
- styles
- colours.

Noun phrases:

- the headword
- words that come before the headword
- words that come after the headword
- relative clauses.

Writing about the same thing from two different points of view

Words can't describe it ...

Exercise A

Yuri wants to learn how to describe fashions so that he can do voice-overs for his fashion programme. He has asked Sarah-Jane to describe the jacket that the male model is wearing above. What should she write?

1. List as many words as you can to describe the type of jacket.
2. List as many words as you can to describe the shape.
3. List as many words as you can to describe the colour.
4. Use the words you have collected to write two or three sentences describing the jacket.

Exercise B

Clothing has a lot of special words.

1. Can you write a short explanation of what each of these words means:

   dress ***frock*** ***gown***

2. How many of these can you explain?

   breeches ***cords*** ***culottes***
   dungarees ***flares*** ***jeans***
   jodhpurs ***slacks*** ***trews***

Shades of red

Exercise A

Colours are important in fashion – and so are the names we use to describe them. These are all names of make-up colours. What colour do you think each one describes?

1. Choose one of the names and write one or two sentences describing what colour you think it is.
2. Now do the same for two more of the names.

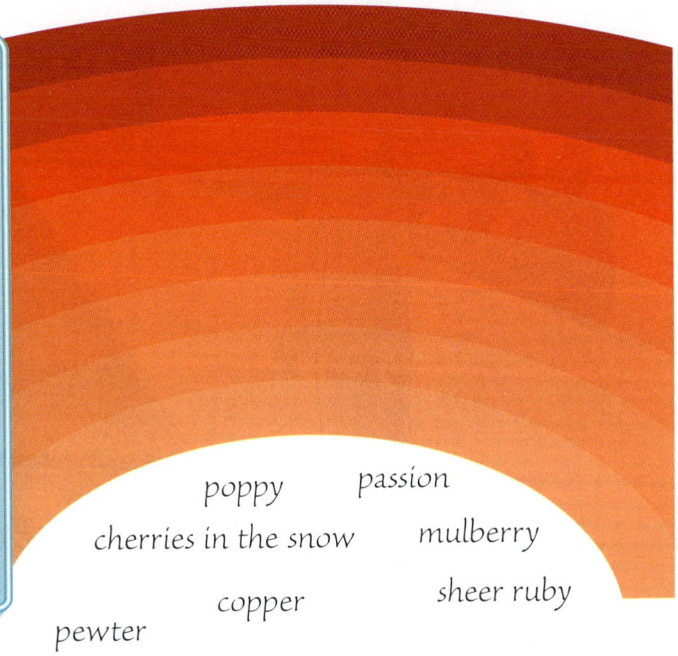

Exercise B

Even if you aren't looking around for 'fashionable' names for colours, there are plenty to choose from. All the words in the list below are used to describe different shades of red:

Words

brick	***cherry***	***coral***
crimson	***magenta***	***maroon***
oxblood	***peach***	***pink***
red	***rose***	***ruby***
salmon	***vermilion***	

1. If there are words in the list you don't know, find out what they mean.
2. Which word in the list describes the darkest red?
3. Which describes the palest?
4. Make a league table:
   a Choose six words from the list.
   b Put the palest word at the top.
   c Put the remaining words in order so that they gradually get darker until you reach the bottom.

Exercise C

How many words can you think of to describe different shades of yellow?

1. Write down all the words you can think of.
2. Choose six and make a league table.

Noun phrases

Exercise A

Explain to Yuri:

1. What a noun phrase is.
2. How we build one up, starting with a noun (the **headword**).

Yuri is using noun phrases* to describe what the model is wearing – but it is taking him a long time to work out how to do it. You can help him by explaining how a noun phrase is built up. Here is an example:

brother

my brother

my older brother

my clumsy infuriating older brother

*** Noun phrases**
If you want to check up on noun phrases, look on page 160.

Exercise B

Build up a noun phrase on each of the following headwords:

1. sister
2. teacher
3. film
4. day
5. car

Exercise C

For each of the noun phrases you have made up, write a sentence using it correctly and underline the phrase. For example:

I've just had a big row with <u>my clumsy infuriating older brother</u>.

Before and after the noun

In the example on page 108, all the words we added to the noun headword came before it. Most of them were adjectives (***clumsy, infuriating, older***). You can also add words *after* the headword:

a dress with blue sleeves

a dress in red and yellow silk

a dress from the fashion house of Chanel

Exercise A

The headword of each of those noun phrases is 'dress'. Look at the words that come after it. Each one is a phrase beginning with a particular kind of word.

1. What kind of word is it?
2. So what kind of phrase is used in each example?
3. Make up a noun phrase of your own. Use the noun ***shirt*** as the headword. Add a phrase after the headword similar to those used in the examples.

Relative clauses

We can build up noun phrases in another way. Look at this example:

Who is that man?

Who is that man over there?

Who is that man who is standing in the corner?

In the last sentence, the group of words that comes after 'man' is like a little sentence itself. It has a subject, 'who', and a verb, 'is standing'. It is called a **relative clause**. Relative clauses come after nouns and begin with words like 'who' and 'that'.

Exercise B

In each of these sentences, some words are underlined. Replace them with a relative clause starting with 'who' or 'that'.

1. Where is that letter <u>from Jane</u>?
2. She is the woman <u>from next door</u>.
3. That's the bus <u>to Battersea</u>.
4. Mr Jones is the man <u>for the job</u>.

Using noun phrases

Read the text and then do the exercises.

___1___ was the 18th century style victim, George Bryan Brummel – but you can call him 'Beau'. Beau was what is known as a dandy or a fop – that's ___2___. He was a real trendsetter of his day and even ___3___ came to him for fashion tips.

Beau was particularly nuts about cravats and started a fashion for wearing them tied in large and complicated knots ('Beau' ties?). His own cravat had to be absolutely perfect before he would even step outside his front door. If he didn't manage to tie it perfectly first time he would sniff haughtily and toss it to one side, pick up another and start all over again – even if it meant spending all morning just tying cravats (… and sniffing haughtily). And this was all because he wanted to give everyone the impression that he'd just 'thrown on' ___4___ then knotted it in seconds.

In addition to being nuts about ___5___, Beau introduced ___6___ … and having a really good wash before you put them on. Before Beau came along, most fashionable men thought that grooming was something you did to animals – the idea of actually being clean came as something of a surprise to most of them.

Exercise A

As you can see, some noun phrases have been removed from the passage. Which noun phrase should go in which space?

1. Write down the number of each space.
2. Against it write the letter of the phrase that should go in it.

Phrases

A *accessories like cravats*
B *someone who is so obsessed with fashion that their whole life revolves around it*
C *the first cravat that came to hand*
D *some revolutionary men's fashion ideas such as wearing clean clothes*
E *the future King of England*
F *a smashin' fashion fanatic who was wild about fashion accessories*

Exercise B

1. Make a table like the one at the bottom of this page. Write out the six phrases, putting the different sections in the right places. One has been done for you.

Words before the headword	Headword	Words after the headword
the first	cravat	that came to hand

Exercise C

In the text that follows the questions are missing. They are listed at the end in the wrong order, and with some noun phrases missing. Work out what the questions should be and where they should go.

Gabrielle ('Coco') Chanel (1883–1971)

Question 1
Yes, she was abandoned by her dad when she was only 12 and had to go and live in an orphanage.

Question 2
While she was working as a dressmaker a few years later she met a fabulously wealthy man and went to live with him on his magnificent country estate. With a bit of help from his dosh and her own talent for design she was able to start her own fashion business. It was called Chanel Modes.

Question 3
She was. She became famous for something known as 'classic chic'.

Question 4
It means using fashion simply but effectively rather than going completely over the top.

Question 5
She most certainly wasn't! She much preferred simple fashions like collarless cardigan suits worn with carefully chosen costume jewellery.

Question 6
During the early 1960s she came up with a little black dress that immediately became top of the frocks. It was known as …

Question 7
You took the words right out of my wardrobe. Yes, every woman was supposed to have one of these dresses as a standby for those special occasions like cocktail parties, unexpected dinner invitations …

Questions

- *Don't tell me, '_______'?*
- *Hmmm, very posh! She sounds like _______?*
- *What's that when it's at home?*
- *Is it true she had _______?*
- *So how did she get to be _______?*
- *So she wasn't into _______?*
- *What was she most famous for?*

Missing phrases

- *the little black dress*
- *a stylish character*
- *nine-inch platform soles and star-spangled cat suits*
- *a rough start in life*
- *a smashin' fashion superstar*

Fashion or anti-fashion?

There is always more than one way of describing something. Fashion and clothing often produce very different reactions in people. For example, you can describe an outfit:

- with enthusiasm, using all the 'right' words

or

- in a no-nonsense, down-to-earth, debunking way.

Exercise A

1. Look at the outfit in picture 1 on page 113.
2. You are going to write a paragraph about it for a fashion magazine. Make a list of words to use to describe:
   - the type of garments
   - the materials
   - the cuts
   - the colours.
3. Now use your notes to write a paragraph describing the fashion. **Remember: you are an enthusiast writing for enthusiasts!**

Exercise B

Imagine that you are Gofer and have just seen the man in picture 1 walking down the street near your school. One of your friends sees you and asks, 'What were you staring at just now?' You are going to write your reply.

1. Look at the lists of words you made for Exercise A. For each list (material, colours, etc.) make a list of words that have a similar meaning but make clear what you really think of the fashion – not a lot!
2. Use your notes to write a paragraph in answer to your friend's question.

Summing up what you've learned

The language of fashion

Fashion and clothing are a good example of a subject that has a lot of specialist words:

- for garments
- for the shape and cut of clothes
- for colours.

Some of these words are **technical terms**. For example:

chiffon
waistcoat
twill

Other words and phrases are made up by designers and advertisers to make things sound attractive. This is especially true of names for colours:

cherries in the snow
shameful red

When we read fashion writing we have to remember that it is all about selling clothes – and is mainly a special kind of advertising!

Noun phrases

A noun phrase can have three main parts:

1. the headword
2. words that come before the headword
3. words that come after the headword.

a blue	*dress*	*with short sleeves*
BEFORE	HEADWORD	AFTER

Before the headword

There are two main kinds of word that come before the headword:

1. *a*, *an*, *the* (these are called articles), other words like *all*, *some*, *any*, *most*, *my*, *his*, *her*, and all numbers
2. adjectives that tell us more about the noun.

After the headword

There are two very common groups of words that can come after the headword:

1. phrases beginning with a preposition (*the man <u>in the bowler hat</u>*)
2. relative clauses (*the man <u>who was wearing a bowler hat</u>*).

UNIT 12

The specialists

Yuri has asked a group of people of your age to tell him what they do in their spare time. He wants to make a programme about 'leisure pursuits'.

- Look at the people in the picture. What spare-time activities can you see there?
- Are these all typical spare-time interests for people of your age?
- What could you add to the list?

In this unit you will learn about:

Writing about specialist subjects:

- using and explaining technical terms
- the 'Who?', 'Why?' and 'How?' of writing.

Prefixes and suffixes:

- some common prefixes and what they mean
- some common suffixes and how they are used.

Planning and scripting a short TV programme

Talking specialist

Yuri has asked Sarah-Jane to find him some background information about specialist interests – but he can't understand a word of it!

Read the texts and then look at the exercise.

A

Ask your instructor if you can have some lessons on the lungeing rein. The instructor will attach a long rein to a special piece of tack called a lunge cavesson and use this to tell the pony when to trot, walk and stop.

B

When you've landed a few successful 50-50s, try to see if you can make a 5-0. Approach the kerb as you would for the 50-50, ollie onto the edge but land just on the back truck and grind along with the nose pointing upwards in a manual.

C

Starting from a *demi-plié* in fifth, with your arms in third (same arm as leg in front of you), spring up into the air drawing the legs together and bringing your outstretched arm into first. Use your spotting technique to turn a full circle *en dehors*, bringing your back leg to the front, and landing in a smooth fifth *demi-plié*.

Exercise A

For each of the three texts, write down the answers to these questions:

1. What activity do you think the text is describing?
2. What makes you think this?
3. Write down any specialist words used in the text. Against each one put a tick if you think you know what it means, and a cross if you don't.

Which of the texts do you find easiest to follow – and why?

Introductions

The texts on the previous page were taken from the middle of the books they came from. You would have found them much easier to understand if you had read the rest of the book! Here's how two of the books started:

A

Do you know how to make friends with a pony or jump a course of fences? Perhaps you dream of being an Olympic showjumper or simply long to gallop a pony along the beach. Whatever your ambition, this is the book for you. Find out how to choose a riding school, get the most from your lessons and tackle your first jump. There are masses of practical tips, plus info on breeds, tack, pony care and the stars of the horse world. If you're not pony mad already, you soon will be!

B

Visit any city anywhere in the world, and you're bound to find a bunch of skaters jumping, sliding and grinding the local terrain as hard as they can. And it doesn't matter where you are or who you are, if you can ride (or almost ride) a board, they'll make you welcome. The skateboard spirit is universal – you've got friends out there you never knew you had!

But how do you ride with style? How do you kickturn, pull ollies and airs? What's the secret to successfully carrying off slick tricks on mini-ramps and verts? And is it really possible to make a career from skateboarding? To find out and to become a member of the coolest club in the world, read on … and enjoy the ride of your life!

Exercise A

Read the two texts and then answer these questions about each of them.

1. **Who?**
   What kind of person is the writer addressing, and what makes you think so?
2. **Why?**
   What is the writer's main purpose in writing – what effect does he or she want to have on the reader?
3. **How?**
   What kind of writing is this: story, description, explanation, argument/persuasion, or a mixture?
4. **Words**
   How many technical terms does the writer use? What effect do these have on the reader?

Prefixes

Exercise A

1. Choose one of the prefixes in this table:

Prefix	Examples
bi-	***bicycle, biplane***
mono-	***monocycle, monoplane***
un-	***unable, untie***
under-	***underarm, undercover***

2. Break the examples for the prefix into a prefix and a stem.
3. Explain how the prefix alters or adds to the meaning of the stem.
4. Think of another word that starts with the same prefix.
5. Now do the same for the other three prefixes.

Reminder: the prefix is the part of the word that comes before the stem:

sub	+	***marine***
PREFIX	+	STEM

Exercise B

Work in the same way on these prefixes.

Prefix	Examples
anti-	***anti-clockwise, anti-social***
counter-	***counter-attack, counter-balance***
mis-	***misunderstand, mislead***
semi-	***semi-circle, semi-precious***

Suffixes

Prefixes come before the stem and add to or change the meaning of the stem. Suffixes come after the stem and help us to make new words from old. We can turn nouns into adjectives:

shame + less = shameless

and adjectives into nouns:

happy + ness = happiness

Exercise A

Look at the list of words below and then answer the questions.

beautify *falsify* *horrify*
mystify *prettify* *solidify*

1. What is the suffix in all these words?
2. They all belong to same class of words (same part of speech). What is it?
3. Each of the words is linked to one or more similar words. For example, 'mystify' is linked to 'mystery' and 'mystic'. Write down each of the words in the list and beside it write the word or words it is linked to.
4. Look at all the words and then write an explanation of what **'-ify'** means when we put it at the end of a word.
5. Write down as many more words as you can that end with the same suffix.

Exercise B

Now go through the same steps for these words:

northwards *homewards*
outwards *leftwards*
backwards

Exercise C

Now go through the same steps for these words:

clockwise *lengthwise*
crabwise *otherwise*
likewise

Using prefixes and suffixes

Exercise A

1. In the *Wordkit* there are five prefixes and ten stems. Use each prefix twice and each stem once to make ten words.

2. In the *Wordkit* there are three suffixes and six stems. Use each suffix twice and each stem once to make six words.

Wordkit

Prefixes	Stems		Stems		Suffixes
anti-	*centenary*	*climax*	*class*	*clock*	*-ify*
bi-	*darkness*	*final*	*cross*	*home*	*-ward*
counter-	*focal*	*foil*	*north*	*simpl(e)*	*-wise*
mono-	*freeze*	*part*			
semi-	*rail*	*tone*			

Exercise B

1. Each of the following nine sentences has a word missing. Use one of the words you have made in Exercise A to fill each gap. Write the letter of the sentence and the word that should go in the gap.

2. You should have seven words left over. Write your own sentence for each of them.

Sentences

A *Complete both sides of the form, hand the large part to the receptionist and keep the ______.*

B *The new trains at the Exhibition are unusual because they run on a ______.*

C *Dad wears ______ spectacles.*

D *She was very embarrassed and spoke in a ______.*

E *I played in goal and my ______ in the opposing team was very good.*

F *This year the school is celebrating its ______.*

G *If you can't swim a length of the bath, the school will _____ you as a non-swimmer.*

H *The pattern ran _____ rather than from top to bottom.*

I *When we crossed the Channel to France it was very rough but on the _____ journey the sea was calm.*

Building in explanations

Yuri's TV programme has to be understood by everyone, so any special words and phrases have to be explained. It's no use telling viewers things like those on page 116! Perhaps you can help.

Exercise A

Use the information sheet to write a short explanation of what an *assemblé derrière* is and how it is done. Remember that you are writing for people who are interested in the subject but have no specialist knowledge.

Assemblé

This is a type of jump that starts from one foot, but lands on both. It can be done in different directions and can also be done with a change of feet 'over' and 'under'.

For an *assemblé derrière*, begin in fifth *demi-plié* with your back foot *sur le cou de pied* (1). Use your *battement frappé* to strike through the floor, stretching your leg out to second and lifting you in the air (2). Stretch your supporting leg underneath you as you lift up and travel (3). Just before you land, bring both legs together (same foot in front), then lower into a *demi-plié* (4).

Glossary

demi-plié — a half knee bend in one of the five positions of the feet

battement frappé — an exercise in which you stand on one leg and strike the floor with the other

second, fifth — different positions of the feet when standing

sur le cou de pied — a position in which the working foot rests on or around the supporting ankle

Special interest TV

Yuri has asked Sarah-Jane to come up with ideas for his programme about special interest activities. The programme will contain a number of short sections about different activities – like riding and skateboarding. These are the details:

Audience

People aged 12–16

Purpose

To entertain them, to give them information about the activity and to persuade them that it is interesting and worth trying for themselves.

Yuri wants a commentary and suggestions about what he should film. He wants the following:

1. A paragraph introducing the activity.
2. Three paragraphs describing the most interesting and important things about it.
3. As each paragraph is spoken, there will be one or more film shots showing something happening. You have to decide which shots you want and describe what each one will show.

Exercise A

1. Choose an activity that you are interested in and know something about.
2. Make a list of five or six things that make that activity interesting and enjoyable.
3. Look at the list and pick the three features that you think are most important.
4. Choose one of the three. Make a list of points that back it up.
5. Use your notes to write a paragraph about your chosen feature.

Rock Climbing

1 open air – healthy
2 needs a lot of skill
3 exciting but safe
4 meet interesting people
5 go to interesting places
6 can practise at Leisure Centre

1 EXCITING
2 HEALTHY
3 SKILFUL

EXCITING
- you against the mountain
- often high up and very exposed
- responsible for your own safety
- need to concentrate all the time

Exercise B

Now think about the film shots you want to accompany your paragraph. Remember that the words don't have to be spoken continuously – there will be pauses while the viewer concentrates on what is on the screen. List three or four shots to include.

Exercise C

Now follow the same steps to write paragraphs about your other two features. Make a list of film shots for each of these.

Exercise D

Finish your commentary off by writing an introductory paragraph. If you want guidance on style look at the two introductions on page 117. When you have written it, make a list of film shots to go with it.

Summing up what you've learned

Specialist writing

When you write about a specialist subject, you have to think carefully about your audience:

- How much do they know about the subject?
- How much do you need to explain?
- What special or technical words do you need to explain?
- How do you do this?

Prefixes

Common prefixes include:

Prefix	Meaning	Examples
anti-	*against*	*anti-clockwise, anti-social*
bi-	*two*	*bicycle, biplane*
counter-	*against*	*counter-attack, counter-balance*
mis-	*opposite of, not*	*misunderstand, mislead*
mono-	*one*	*monocycle, monoplane*
semi-	*half*	*semi-circle, semi-precious*
un-	*not, opposite of*	*unable, untie*
under-	*under*	*underarm, undercover*

Suffixes

Common suffixes include:

Suffix	Use	Examples
-ify	*makes a noun or adjective into a verb*	*beautify, falsify*
-ward(s)	*makes another word into an adverb meaning 'in the direction of'*	*northward(s), backward(s)*
-wise	*makes another word into an adverb (some -wise words can also be used as adjectives)*	*clockwise, otherwise*

UNIT 13

Yuri's tour of Britain

Yuri has decided to make a programme to show viewers in Herzegovina some of the sights of Britain.

- Where do you think he should go?
- If he came to the area you live in, where should he visit?
- Some people say that tourists shouldn't just be shown historical and 'pretty-pretty' places. Do you agree? If so, what else should they visit?

In this unit you will learn about:

Travel writing:
- different kinds of writing
- who reads it
- the information it can provide.

Simple and multiple sentences:
- joining simple sentences in different ways
- avoiding using 'and' too much.

Vocabulary:
- how to avoid using words that are too simple and obvious
- how to choose more interesting and accurate words.

What kind of information?

Sarah-Jane has collected a lot of texts about different tourist places Yuri could use for the programme. The texts provide different kinds of information.

Exercise A

Read the three texts on this page. For each one write two or three sentences commenting on:

- **a** the kind of information it contains
- **b** the way in which it is written
- **c** the audience it is written for
- **d** how useful Yuri will find it.

A

DURHAM, a maritime county and its former county town, in north-eastern England, along the North Sea coast.

The City. Durham is centred on a rocky peninsula in a loop of the River Wear. Its cathedral was begun in 1093, and Durham's castle was erected by William the Conqueror.

B

I was heading for Newcastle, by way of York, when I did another impetuous thing. I got off at Durham, intending to poke around the cathedral for an hour or so and fell in love with it instantly in a serious way.

The cathedral, a mountain of reddish-brown stone high above a lazy green loop of the River Wear, is, of course, its glory. Everything about it was perfect – not just its setting and execution but also, no less notably, the way it is run today. For a start there was no nagging for money, no 'voluntary' admission fee. Inside, there were two modest collecting boxes and nothing else to detract from the unutterable soaring majesty of the interior. It was a perfect day to see it. Sun slanted lavishly through the stained-glass windows, highlighting the stout pillars with their sumptuously grooved patterns and spattering the floors with motes of colour.

C

Surrounded on three sides by the River Wear, Durham's surprisingly compact centre is readily approached by two small bridges which lead from the western, modern part of town across the river to the spur containing castle and cathedral. The commercial heart of this 'old town' area is the triangular Market Place.

From Market Place it's a five-minute walk up the steep and cobbled Sadler street to the majestic Durham Cathedral facing the castle across the manicured Palace Green. Standing on the site of an early wooden Saxon cathedral, built to house the remains of St Cuthbert, the present cathedral – the work of French master masons – was completed in 1133.

Exercise B

Read the text below and then answer these questions.

1. If you had to give this text a title (not just 'Blackpool'!) what would you call it?
2. Sum up the author's attitude to Blackpool in two or three sentences.
3. Do you think the author makes a good case for his opinion? What are your reasons?
4. Does he say any positive things about Blackpool? If so, give examples.

Blackpool – and I don't care how many times you hear this, it never stops being amazing – attracts more visitors every year than Greece and has more holiday beds than Portugal. It consumes more chips per capita than anywhere else on the planet. (It gets through 40 acres of potatoes a day.) It has the largest concentration of rollercoasters in Europe. It has the continent's second most popular tourist attraction, the 42-acre Pleasure Beach, whose 6.5 million annual visitors are only exceeded by those going to the Vatican. It has the most famous illuminations. And on Friday and Saturday nights it has more public toilets than anywhere else in Britain; elsewhere they call them doorways.

Whatever you may think of the place, it does what it does very well – or if not very well at least very successfully. In the past twenty years, during a period in which the number of Britons taking traditional seaside holidays has declined by a fifth, Blackpool has increased its visitor numbers by 7 per cent and built tourism into a £250-million-a-year industry – no small achievement when you consider the British climate, the fact that Blackpool is ugly, dirty and a long way from anywhere, that its sea is an open toilet, and its attractions nearly all cheap, provincial and dire.

It was the illuminations that had brought me there. I had been hearing and reading about them for so long that I was genuinely keen to see them. So after securing a room in a modest guesthouse on a back street, I hastened to the front in a sense of some expectation. Well, all I can say is that Blackpool's illuminations are nothing if not splendid, and they are not splendid. There is, of course, always a danger of disappointment when you finally encounter something you have wanted to see for a long time, but in terms of letdown it would be hard to exceed Blackpool's light show. I thought there would be lasers sweeping the sky, strobe lights tattooing the clouds and other gasp-making dazzlements. Instead there was just a rumbling procession of old trams decorated as rocket ships or Christmas crackers, and several miles of paltry decorations on lampposts. I suppose if you had never seen electricity in action, it would be pretty breathtaking, but I'm not even sure of that. It all just seemed tacky and inadequate on rather a grand scale, like Blackpool itself.

Joining up

Yuri has at last got the hang of writing simple sentences in English. He has made a start on the script of his travel programme. Sarah-Jane doesn't think much of it.

> Stratford-upon-Avon
>
> Stratford-upon-Avon is in Warwickshire.
> Stratford-upon-Avon was the birthplace of William Shakespeare.
> Shakespeare was a famous English writer.

Sarah-Jane told Yuri he was writing too many short sentences. So he wrote a second version:

> Stratford-upon-Avon
>
> Stratford-upon-Avon is in Warwickshire and was the birthplace of William Shakespeare and Shakespeare was a famous English writer.

Exercise A

See if you can do better. Make Yuri's three sentences into one without using 'and'.

Different kinds of sentence

Sentences that have one subject and one verb are called **simple sentences.** If we join two (or more) simple sentences together, we make a **multiple sentence:**

Stratford-upon-Avon is in Warwickshire. + ***It was the birthplace of William Shakespeare.***

SIMPLE SENTENCE → MULTIPLE SENTENCE ← SIMPLE SENTENCE

Stratford-upon-Avon is in Warwickshire and was the birthplace of William Shakespeare.

We can join simple sentences together using these words, called **conjunctions:**

and ***but*** ***or/nor*** ***then***

They work like 'plus' signs in maths and add sentences together. If you make too many multiple sentences, especially using 'and', your writing will become very boring.

Choices

These three sentences can be joined together in a number of different ways, without using 'and' more than once.

Shakespeare was a famous English writer.
He lived from 1564 to 1616.
He wrote 37 plays.

- Shakespeare was a famous English writer who lived from 1564 to 1616 and wrote 37 plays.
- Shakespeare, who lived from 1564 to 1616, was a famous English writer and wrote 37 plays.
- The famous English writer Shakespeare who lived from 1564 to 1616 wrote 37 plays.

Exercise A

Join each of these groups of sentences into one multiple sentence. Try to avoid using 'and' at all – and never use it more than once in any sentence.

1. There are many places to visit in Stratford.
   There are three theatres.
   They all belong to the Royal Shakespeare Company.
2. The main theatre was designed by Elisabeth Scott.
   It is used for performances of Shakespeare's plays.
   It is on the bank of the River Avon.
3. The Swan Theatre is next door.
   It is like a sixteenth-century theatre.
   It also contains a bookshop.
4. The third theatre is called 'The Other Place'.
   It is much smaller than the other two.
   It is mainly used for modern plays.
5. Thousands of people visit Stratford every year.
   Many of them come from overseas.
   Stratford is particularly popular with Americans.

Exercise B

All the groups of sentences in Exercise A can be joined together in more than one way. Write a second set of multiple sentences joining them in a different way. Again, do not use 'and' more than once in each sentence.

Twenty sentences

Yuri still hasn't got the hang of joining sentences up. He's done some research about things to do at Blackpool, but needs help in writing it up.

Exercise A

Below are the first seven sentences Yuri wrote. They are all fairly short. Your job is to combine them into a smaller number of longer sentences. You should be able to put all this information into no more than four sentences – or even three. Don't use 'and' more than twice.

1. Blackpool has seven miles of beach and a promenade.
2. The tide ebb is a full half a mile.
3. It leaves plenty of sand at low tide.
4. The major event is Blackpool's Pleasure Beach on the South Promenade.
5. The South Promenade is just south of South Pier.
6. Entrance to the amusement park is free.
7. You'll have to fork out for the superb array of 'white knuckle' rides.

Exercise B

Now do the same with these sentences. You should be able to reduce the number of sentences to no more than six – or even five. No more than three 'and's!

8. The rides at the Pleasure Beach include The Big One.
9. This is the world's fastest roller-coaster (85 m.p.h.).
10. This involves a terrifying near-vertical drop from 235 feet.
11. The latest thrill is the PlayStation.
12. This whooshes up a 200-ft steel tower at 80 m.p.h.
13. Then it drops you back down in free-fall.
14. You can buy a ticket book (£20).
15. This saves you paying a pound or two a time to ride.
16. The Big One costs £4.
17. The Sandcastle is across the road.
18. It is the only place you are likely to want to swim.
19. Every aquatic diversion is kept at a constant 29°C.
20. It can be a welcome respite from the bracing sea air.

It's really interesting

Yuri doesn't know a lot of adjectives. So when he is writing a description he uses the same tired old adjectives over and over again.

> The city of York is very interesting. The city walls are old and the tour round the walls was really interesting. The Cathedral is very old ...

Exercise A

Help Yuri out here.

1. Make a list of words he could use instead of 'interesting' in those sentences.
2. Make a list of words he could use instead of 'old' in those sentences.

Exercise B

One word people use far too much is 'nice'. Usually when people use it, it just means that they like the person or thing they are describing. There are plenty of other words:

agreeable	*appealing*	*attractive*	*captivating*	*charming*	*delightful*
enjoyable	*exciting*	*fascinating*	*interesting*	*intriguing*	*inviting*
irresistible	*likeable*	*pleasing*	*stimulating*		

1. Read through the list. Write down any words you do not know the meaning of. Find out what they mean.
2. Write down five words from the list that could be used to describe a person.
3. Write down five words from the list that could be used to describe a place.
4. Write five sentences, each one using one of the words in the list.

Exercise C

Now do the same for this list of words:

ample	*big*	*colossal*	*enormous*	*giant*
gigantic	*grand*	*huge*	*immense*	*imposing*
jumbo	*massive*	*monumental*	*roomy*	*spacious*
substantial	*tall*	*towering*	*whopping*	

Love it or hate it?

Gofer and Sarah-Jane clearly don't agree about Blackpool. You can probably think of places that you love and other places you can't stand. In this writing exercise you have the chance to be completely biased and unfair about a place.

Exercise A

1. Think of a place you do not like at all.
2. Copy and complete this sentence:
   If there's one place I cannot stand it's __(name)__.
3. Copy and complete this sentence:
   The worst thing about __(name)__ *is* ________________.
4. Copy and complete this sentence:
   The worst time to visit __(name)__ *is* ________________,
   because ________________.

Exercise B

The purpose of writing those three sentences was to get your mind working on the place you have chosen. Now make a list of all the things you really hate about the place. Don't worry about writing complete sentences; just jot down all the ideas you can think of.

Exercise C

Now you are going to plan four paragraphs:

1. introducing the place and your feelings about it
2. describing the main things you dislike about the place
3. focusing on one particular thing about it that stands out in your mind
4. summing up your feelings – possibly with advice for the person about to visit this place.

Use the notes that you made for Exercise B and add any other ideas you think of. Make a list of the points you want to include in each paragraph.

Exercise D

Use your plan and write the four paragraphs.

Summing up what you've learned

Travel writing

There are different kinds of travel writing. Two common ones are:

Guide books

These are written for people who are thinking of visiting the place described. They give factual information about:

- what to see
- where to eat and drink
- where to stay

as well as background information about the place and its history.

Personal accounts

These describe a journey taken by the writer. They often contain a lot of information about places, but they usually also give the writer's thoughts and feelings about the places. They are written to entertain the reader.

Simple and multiple sentences

Simple sentences contain one subject and one verb. A sentence that contains more than one verb is a **multiple sentence**.

These are examples of **simple sentences**:

Stratford-upon-Avon is in Warwickshire.
It was the birthplace of William Shakespeare.

These are examples of **multiple sentences**:

Stratford-upon-Avon is in Warwickshire and it was the birthplace of William Shakespeare.
Stratford-upon-Avon, which is in Warwickshire, was the birthplace of William Shakespeare.

Multiple sentences

You can turn simple sentences into multiple sentences by joining them with the **conjunction** 'and':

Stratford-upon-Avon is in Warwickshire and it was the birthplace of William Shakespeare.

Other words that can be used in the same way are:

but *or/nor* *then*

If you use 'and' too much to join sentences, your writing will become boring:

It was a school holiday on Monday and the weather was fine and we decided to go down to the river and we took a picnic and we went in the car...

The Big Debate

Yuri's stay in Britain is coming towards its end. He has decided to stage a studio debate in which people from all over Britain debate what is good and bad about living there. These are the questions the guests will be asked:

- What do you think are the best things about living in Britain?
- What are the worst things?
- If you had to live abroad what would you miss most?
- And what would you be happiest to get away from?

In this unit you will learn about:

Expressing opinions and stating arguments

Using conjunctions to link sentences

Using adverbials to show how sentences work together

Organizing and building up an argument in five paragraphs

The British

Yuri has tried very hard to understand the British. He asked Sarah-Jane to find him some books to help him, but he still needs help. Read these extracts carefully and then look at the instructions in Exercise A.

A

The English are addicted to cheese. But they detest garlic, a vegetable associated with foreigners, who are held in more or less universal contempt and are the main butts of the jokes which the English like telling to each other. These jokes are bartered in public places, and they increase in value as they grow older and more familiar. For the English are very famous – at least among themselves – for their sense of humour and pronounce it an essential component of a sterling character.

B

The British sense of humour is varied and unpredictable, ranging from a liking for jokes that many (nationals as well as visitors) would regard as racist, sexist, vulgar or lavatorial, to a taste for puns and other plays on words … Shrugging off disappointments with a joke reflects the British cultivation of unflappability: the stiff upper lip.

C

The great English characteristic is the ability to leave you alone, to let you live your own life. My mother said to me that England was the best place to be poor. There is a basic decency here which I have never found anywhere else. Against that, the English are extraordinarily hypocritical. They have a distinct streak of 'holier than thou'.

When I return to England from abroad I am, these days, struck by the shabbiness. But I also immediately realise how much better, and how much safer, how much more courteous the driving is here. I'm always glad to be back … I think it's a decent country, the most decent country in the world, it allows you to live decently with a fair degree of privacy.

Exercise A

Answer these questions about each text.

1. Yuri wants to know: does the writer like the British, or not?
2. What makes you think so?
3. Do you think what the writer is saying is true?
4. What is your opinion of this aspect of the British?

What I love about Britain

This is a longer extract Sarah-Jane found for Yuri.
What does this writer think about Britain and the British?

Suddenly, in the space of a moment, I realised what it was that I loved about Britain – which is to say, all of it. Every last bit of it, good and bad – Marmite, village fêtes, country lanes, people saying 'mustn't grumble' and 'I'm terribly sorry but', people apologising to *me* when I conk them with a careless elbow, milk in bottles, beans on toast, haymaking in June, stinging nettles, seaside piers, Ordnance survey maps, crumpets, hot-water bottles as a necessity, drizzly Sundays – every bit of it.

What a wondrous place this was. What other country, after all, could possibly have come up with place names like Tooting Bec and Farleigh Wallop, or a game like cricket that goes on for three days and never seems to start? Who else would think it not the least odd to make their judges wear little mops on their heads, compel the Lord Chancellor to sit on something called the Woolsack, or take pride in a naval hero whose dying wish was to be kissed by a fellow named Hardy? What other nation in the world would have given us William Shakespeare, pork pies, Christopher Wren, Windsor Great Park, the Open University, *Gardeners' Question Time*, and the chocolate digestive biscuit? None, of course.

How easily we lose sight of this. What an enigma [puzzle] Britain will seem to historians when they look back on the second half of the twentieth century. Here is a country that fought and won a noble war, dismantled a mighty empire in a generally benign [generous] and enlightened way, created a far-seeing welfare state – in short did nearly everything right – and then spent the rest of the century looking on itself as a chronic failure. The fact is that this is still the best place in the world for most things – to post a letter, go for a walk, watch television, buy a book, venture out for a drink, go to a museum, use the bank, get lost, seek help, or stand on a hillside and take in a view.

Exercise A

1. The extract is divided into three paragraphs. Each one has a lead sentence which gives us a clear idea what the paragraph is about. Write down the number of each paragraph and its lead sentence. (**Warning:** it isn't always the first sentence in the paragraph.)
2. Each paragraph contains sentences which develop the idea of the lead sentence. Write the number of each paragraph and one sentence which develops the ideas of the lead sentence. Then explain how it does this.
3. For each paragraph say if you agree with the writer and give your reasons.

Joining sentences

Yuri would like more help in understanding **conjunctions**.

Conjunctions

Conjunctions are used to join sentences together. For example:

or ***because*** ***so*** ***although***

Exercise A

Yuri wants to explain what he thinks of the British and why. He has written these four sentences:

1. I have been very happy here.
2. People have made me very welcome.
3. I have made some good programmes.
4. People in my country have become very interested in Britain.

Join sentences 1 and 2 together using one of the conjunctions in the list above Exercise A. Join sentences 3 and 4 together using a different conjunction from the list.

Exercise B

Perhaps you can help Yuri a bit more by giving him some explanations and examples.

1. He would like to know how this word is used: ***because***
   a Write an example sentence showing how it is used.
   b Write an explanation of when we use it.
2. Which of these words can replace ***because*** in your sentence without changing the meaning?
   as ***if*** ***since*** ***unless***
3. Look at the words you did not choose for the last question. Write an example sentence for each one to show Yuri how it is used.

Exercise C

Yuri wants to know how we use these words and phrases:

although ***even if*** ***except that***

1. Write an example sentence for each one.
2. Explain when we use them.

Using sentence adverbials

It would help Yuri if he understood about another group of words we can use to show the links between sentences. So far he has just written down a list of them:

1	therefore	as a result
2	on the other hand	in contrast
3	for example	for instance
4	also in the same way	in addition similarly
5	firstly then	next finally

These words and phrases are called **sentence adverbials.*** You don't use them to join sentences together, but they tell the reader that there's a connection between two sentences:

She wasn't looking where she was going.
As a result she tripped over her own skipping rope.

As you can see, ***therefore*** and ***as a result*** tell the reader that one thing caused the other.

Exercise A

1. Choose one of the other groups of words and write down its number.
2. Choose two words or phrases from the list. For each one write one or two sentences showing how the word or phrase is used.
3. Now write an explanation of what all the words in your chosen group have in common.

Exercise B

Now do the same for another of the groups.

*** Adverbials**

You learned about these in Unit 3 (pages 32–35). The information on this page builds on what you have already learned.

Great mistakes

Exercise A

In this story some of the connecting words – conjunctions and adverbs* – have been missed out. They are listed in the word box. Write down the number of each blank and the word that should go in it.

Word box

as	*before*	*how*
however	*or*	*then*
until	*when*	
as an example		
within minutes		

Committing the perfect crime and getting away scot-free is a difficult task. What with police detectives, forensic scientists, psychological profilers, and psychics on their trail, you might think that criminals would have a tough enough time already.

Some lawbreakers, ___1___, can't help making things even harder for themselves.

___2___, consider the case of John Roberts from Pennsylvania, USA. Roberts spent over a week planning a bank robbery in the summer of 1994. He took care to work out what kind of mask he would wear, how much money he could carry, and what his best getaway route would be.

___3___ he finally put his plan into action, the raid went like clockwork and bank staff filled up his bag ___4___ it was brimming with used cash. Roberts made staff and customers lie on the floor, ___5___ left the building before police arrived.

Having made sure that he was not being followed, Roberts slipped back to his apartment and paused to count the money ___6___ skipping town for good.

___7___ there was a knock at the door and Roberts found himself confronted by half a dozen police officers – who promptly arrested him.

Roberts wondered ___8___ they had tracked him down so very quickly. Had someone recognized him under his mask? ___9___ had he been followed from the bank after all? Police pointed to his jacket, now lying across the back of a chair, and Roberts realised his mistake.

He had worn his favourite jacket for the robbery, ___10___ he did for all important occasions. Embroidered across its back, in large letters, was his name 'John Edward Roberts'.

*** Adverbs**

You learned about these in Unit 4 (pages 42–45). The adverbs used on this page are single words that are being used as sentence adverbials.

Exercise B

This story is told as a series of simple sentences. There are 26 of them! Rewrite part of it.

1. Choose a group of six or seven sentences.
2. Combine the sentences so that there are fewer of them and make that part of the story more interesting to read.
3. You should be able to do it in no more than three sentences.

1 The first psychological profile ever used in a police investigation was created by Dr James Brussel in 1957.

2 Dr Brussel was a leading psychiatrist.

3 He worked for New York State's Mental Health Department.

4 The police asked Dr Brussel to try to assist them in their hunt for the 'Mad Bomber'.

5 He was an unknown man.

6 He had been terrorising the city of New York for sixteen years.

7 He had been leaving home-made bombs in public places.

8 Detectives knew that the Mad Bomber was pursuing a one-man vendetta against a company.

9 The company was called Consolidated Edison.

10 They had no idea of his identity.

11 Dr Brussel was a psychiatrist.

12 He already knew that he could study a man's mind.

13 He could make reasonably accurate predictions about how that person would behave.

14 Dr Brussel made a great leap.

15 He reasoned that he could also do the reverse.

16 He could look at a man's behaviour (in the case of the Mad Bomber, his crimes).

17 He could make deductions about his character.

18 He could make deductions about his identity.

19 Dr Brussel went through the police's case file on the bomber.

20 He produced a profile of the bomber.

21 Altogether his profile ran to seventeen major points about the bomber.

22 Police studied it carefully.

23 Soon after the bomber gave himself away.

24 He was arrested.

25 His name was George Metesky.

26 Dr Brussel's profile of the bomber was an exact match of George Metesky in thirteen out of the seventeen categories.

The big debate

Yuri has asked for contributions to the debate about what is good and bad about living in Britain. Everyone who wants to take part has to send in a written argument with an introduction, three main paragraphs, and a conclusion.

Exercise A

Choose a lead sentence from the Word bank opposite, or write your own. Use it to start a paragraph expressing some of your views about the topic. Use the Word bank to help you.

Exercise B

Now choose or make up two more lead sentences and write a paragraph for each.

Exercise C

Look at your three paragraphs and put them in the best order. Write a short paragraph to introduce them.

Exercise D

Think of a good way of finishing your argument. Write a concluding paragraph that sums up your feelings.

Word bank

Conjunctions

or	*because*
so	*although*
since	*unless*
even if	*except that*
as if	

Adverbials

therefore	*as a result*
on the one hand	*on the other hand*
in contrast	
for example	*for instance*
also	*in addition*
in the same way	*similarly*
firstly	*next*
then	*finally*

Sentence patterns

You could say that ... but I believe that ...
Some people think ... but others argue that ...

Lead sentences

You cannot beat British ______ ...
If I could, I would emigrate to ______.
I would hate to live anywhere else, because ...
What I cannot stand about living in this country is ...
They say, 'British is best' and I could not agree/disagree more.

Summing up what you've learned

Reading arguments

When we read an argument we can:

- say whether the writer gives reasons for the opinions and beliefs in it
- say whether we think the reasons are good reasons or not
- say if we agree or disagree with the writer.

If you are in a hurry you can often get a good idea of what the writer thinks by just reading the lead sentence of each paragraph – usually the first or second sentence.

Sentence adverbials

These are words and phrases that show how one sentence is connected with another. In these examples the sentence adverbials have been underlined.

I wasn't happy about doing my English homework. Firstly it was all about grammar. Then I hadn't got all the instructions down properly. Finally I'd lost my pen.

She couldn't make up her mind about Mark. On the one hand he seemed pleasant enough. On the other hand he seemed to be very friendly with Tina.

Conjunctions

We can join two simple sentences into a multiple sentence by using conjunctions.

Examples of conjunctions are:

or	*because*	*so*	*although*
as	*if*	*since*	*unless*

Examples of multiple sentences made using conjunctions are:

We can go to see Mrs Mann together or I'll go on my own.

Although it was raining, they still played rounders.

Unless you obey the school rules you'll get into trouble.

Writing an argument

Some advice:

1. Make sure you know what you think!
2. Write in paragraphs.
3. Give each paragraph a good lead sentence that expresses clearly the opinion you want to write about in that paragraph.
4. Always try to give good reasons for your opinions.
5. Begin your argument with a short introductory paragraph and end with a short conclusion.

UNIT 15

Revision unit

This unit reviews some of the language points you have been looking at in Units 11–14.

In this unit you will revise:

Different kinds of writing:

- **who** they are for
- **why** they were written
- **where** they come from
- **how** they are written.

Vocabulary – words for:

- colours
- 'nasty'
- 'small'.

Parts of words:

- how words are made up.

Noun phrases

Adverbials:

- place
- time.

Comparisons

When you are learning a foreign language it is difficult to 'read between the lines'. Often you understand all the words, but you don't understand the whole text completely. Yuri would like some help in understanding *completely* what he reads.

Exercise A

The following texts are both about the same subject matter. Read them carefully and then write answers to these questions:

1. **Who** is each text written for?
2. What is the purpose of each text (**Why**)?
3. What kind of book, magazine or newspaper does each come from (**Where**)?
4. What are the main differences in the way the two texts are written (**How**)?

The trial and execution of Charles I

A

Parliament raised an army … so Charles raised an army. The king's army (the Royalists or Cavaliers) fought the army of Parliament (the Roundheads).

Slimiest acts

Slimy act 1: Parliament wanted Charlie's best pal, Black Tom, executed. Charles said he'd protect Black Tom – within a week of making that promise he signed Black Tom's death warrant.

Slimy act 2: When Charles started to lose the Civil War he made a secret deal with the Scots. They would send an army to help him. The Roundhead leader, Cromwell, was furious! He said this was treason to the English people … and the punishment for treason should be death!

Charlie was one slimy Stuart who tried to be slimy once too often. He lost the war and Parliament sent him to be executed. That put a stop to his slimy games.

B

The king was recaptured and taken to Windsor. The army leaders now realised that they could not trust him. They declared that Charles must be put on public trial for all his wrongdoings.

But most MPs would not allow such a trial; it seemed wrong to do this to a monarch. So, for the first time, the Army turned against Parliament. On 6 December 1648, Colonel Thomas Pride surrounded the House of Commons with soldiers. All MPs were stopped from going in, except those who wanted a trial. The much smaller Parliament appointed a High Court of 135 people. The trial began on 20 January 1649. A week later, Charles I was sentenced to death.

Exercise B

Now answer the same questions for these two texts.

Blenheim Palace Gardens

A

The ornamental garden below one of the terraces at Blenheim Palace is the work of the French garden designer Achille Duchêne. The 9th Duke of Marlborough commissioned Duchêne to create the formal garden with its parterres (level areas with flower beds), ponds and fountains – re-creating the original concept of the garden by Henry Wise, which was destroyed by Capability Brown in his quest for the 'natural garden'.

Under Brown's direction the grounds were transformed into a charming landscape of trees, woods and grass.

B

Beneath an imposing ornamental arch there was a ticket booth and a sign saying that admission for an adult was £6.90, though closer inspection revealed that this included entrance to the palace tour, butterfly house, miniature train, adventure playground and a whole cornucopia of other cultural diversions. Lower down, the sign noted that admission to the grounds alone was 90p. I may be easily fooled but nobody takes 90p from me without good reason. I had a trusty Ordnance Survey map and could see that this was a public right of way, so I strode through the gate with a sneer and my hand on my wallet, and the man in the ticket booth wisely decided not to tamper with me.

Exercise C

Now answer the same questions for these two texts.

Fine tailoring – fine style

A

This season's 'must' – a grey pinstripe suit, from only £150

Single-breasted jacket with concealed button fastening, inset sleeves, button cuff and two-way pockets. Semi-tailored parallel trousers with welt pockets, side zip fastening and slits at the ankles. Available in two leg lengths – 30in or 32in. 21in length pencil skirt with back vent and zip fastening. All in 55% polyester and 45% wool, lined in 100% satin acetate, dry clean only. Sizes 8–16. 100% British designed and manufactured by Emma Hartley.

B

In the 19th century, when cashmere was first introduced to Europe, we clothed our children in it. It wasn't until the 1920s, with the invention of the now ubiquitous [found everywhere] twinset, that cashmere became a staple wardrobe item. Perhaps for the first time since then, cashmere is enjoying mass popularity. As shamelessly indulgent fabrics engulfed the Autumn/Winter 1998 catwalks – mohair, astrakhan, silk-velvet and fur pelts – cashmere revealed itself in many different guises: triple-layered, paper-thin, lightly ribbed, and blended with silk or mohair. Even the high street is now riddled with the stuff.

Colours and sizes

Exercise A

We often describe the shade of a colour by adding a word before it and joining the two with a hyphen:

rose-red ***salmon-pink***

All the words that follow can be used to describe shades of blue or green. Divide them into two lists, 'blue' and 'green'.

grass- ***ice-*** ***leaf-*** ***lime-*** ***midnight-***
olive- ***pea-*** ***powder-*** ***sky-*** ***steel-***

Exercise B

The words that follow are all shades of:

red ***blue*** ***green*** ***purple***

Divide them into four lists with those colours as headings.

aquamarine ***aubergine*** ***azure*** ***cerise***
crimson ***emerald*** ***indigo*** ***jade***
puce ***sapphire*** ***vermilion*** ***violet***

Exercise C

When people want to describe something unpleasant, they often just choose the word 'nasty', but there are plenty of other words they could choose. For example:

annoying ***displeasing*** ***offensive*** ***repulsive*** ***trying***

1. Write down as many more words as you can think of that mean 'nasty'.
2. Make a league table of your list with the least nasty at the top and the most nasty at the bottom.

Exercise D

1. Make a list of all the words you can think of that mean 'small'.
2. Put your words into a league table with the biggest at the top and the smallest at the bottom.

Parts of words

Exercise A

Each of these can come at the beginning of a word. They all give clues about the meaning of the whole word:

anti- bi- mis- mono- semi-

1. What are all these parts of words called?
2. Give an example of a word that begins with each one.
3. Explain the clue that each one gives about the meaning of the word.

Exercise B

Each of these can come at the end of a word:

-ify -less -ness -wards -wise

1. What are all these parts of words called?
2. Give an example of a word that ends with each one.
3. Words that end with these parts can be adjectives, nouns, verbs or adverbs. Which is which?

Exercise C

Each of these can come at the beginning of a word. They all give clues about the meaning of the whole word:

arch- as in ***archbishop***
auto- as in ***autobiography***
dis- as in ***disappear***
pro- as in ***pro-British***
ultra- as in ***ultra-rich***

1. Give another example of a word that begins with each one.
2. Explain the clue that each one gives about the meaning of the word.

Revising noun phrases

Exercise A

In the text that follows, some noun phrases have been removed. They are listed on the right.

1. Write down the number of each space.
2. Against it write the letter of the phrase that should go in it.
3. Write down the headword of each of the noun phrases.

Phrases

A *all sorts of colours and styles*
B *damaged feet*
C *a pair of boots with 'air cushioned' soles*
D *pockets of air built into them*
E *skiing accident in 1945*

Walking on air

Having shoes that are really comfortable is really important – especially if you've got __1__. After breaking his foot in a __2__, a German doctor called Klaus Maertens found his ordinary shoes far too uncomfortable to wear so he designed himself __3__. The soles had __4__, rather than being completely solid.

These boots eventually became known as Doc Martens or DMs and were adopted as smashin' fashion footwear by teenagers from the 1960s onwards. Since then they've been produced in __5__.

Exercise B

In the text on the right, some noun phrases have been removed.

1. Write down the number of each space.
2. Against it write a suitable phrase to fill it.
3. Write down the headword of each of the noun phrases.

Fashion shoes that will run and run

Adolf Dassler originally designed his canvas track shoes for __6__ like the world record-breaking athlete Jesse Owens. In the 1940s it was decided that __7__ should be made much stronger, so that they could withstand __8__. Three strips of leather were added to them and the first trainer was born. Adolf's shoe companies later became known as Adidas and Puma – and their shoes are still running!

As well as putting a spring in __9__, a well-made pair of trainers can protect your feet from __10__ – they may even help you to win races or run away from __11__.

Revising adverbials

Exercise A

In the text that follows, a number of groups of words have been missed out. They are listed on the right.

1. Write the number of each space.
2. Against it write the letter of the group of words you have chosen to fill it.

Phrases

A *at night*
B *by the morning*
C *during the Middle Ages*
D *during this outbreak*
E *for five days*
F *in a nearby inn yard*
G *in huge 'plague pits' at the edge of the City*
H *in the spring of 1665*
I *on 2 September 1666*
J *through the crowded and dirty London streets*

'Lord, how empty the streets are, and melancholy, so many poor sick people in the streets, full of sores, and so many sad stories overheard as I walk, everybody talking of this man dead, and that man sick.' So wrote Samuel Pepys in 1665. Two disasters struck London at the beginning of Charles II's reign: the plague of 1665 and the Great Fire of 1666.

The plague broke out __1__. It was bubonic plague, which had killed many people __2__. There was no cure and it swiftly spread __3__.

__4__, men drove carts through the streets, shouting, 'Bring out your dead!' The corpses were collected and buried __5__. Altogether, nearly 100,000 Londoners died __6__. Puritans believed that the plague was God's punishment for Charles's wicked ways.

__7__, a fire started in a bakery in Pudding Lane. A spark lit a pile of hay __8__. The flames swept into warehouses full of oil and candle wax. __9__, the blaze was out of control.

The fire raged __10__, covering most of the City. Nine people died and more than 13,000 houses and 97 churches were destroyed, including St Paul's Cathedral.

Exercise B

All the missing groups of words are **adverbials.** Some answer the question 'When?' and some the question 'Where?'. Divide them into two groups, with the headings 'When?' and 'Where?'.

Yuri's Goodbye Programme

Yuri has been in Britain for nearly a month. He has made a lot of programmes and learned a lot about Britain and the British.

Now it is time for Yuri to make his last programme.

Exercise A

1. Think of aspects of life in this country that Yuri has not covered. Make a list of them.
2. Choose the subject that would make the best programme. Give it a title.
3. List the main points that the programme would cover.
4. You are going to write a letter to Yuri about the programme. Write an introductory paragraph describing briefly the programme you have chosen.

Exercise B

5. Write a second paragraph describing the main points that the programme will cover. Use the list you made earlier.
6. Now think carefully about *why* you chose your subject. List all the reasons.
7. Write a paragraph explaining why this is a good programme to make.
8. Finish with a short paragraph in which you try to persuade Yuri to make the programme.

Grammar reference

On these pages you will find all the grammar that is contained in Book 1 of *The Language Kit*.

Three kinds of sentence

In English there are three main kinds of sentence:

Statement

A statement tells the reader something:

It's pouring with rain.

Question

A question sentence asks for information:

Is it going to rain today?

Directive

A directive sentence tells someone to do something:

Wipe your feet!

More about questions

There are three kinds of question:

1. **Yes/no questions:**
   Would you like a fry-up for breakfast?
2. **Either/or questions:**
   Would you like cereal or a fry-up for breakfast?
   These questions must contain the word 'or'.
3. **Question-word questions:**
   What would you like for breakfast?
   These questions start with one of these words:
   who whom whose what where why when how which

More about directives

Directive sentences are used for several different purposes. The commonest are:

1. To invite
   Come to the film with me tonight.
2. To order or command
   Get out of my way!
3. To beg or plead
   Lend me a pound.
4. To wish someone well
   Have a nice time!
5. To advise
   Take it easy for a bit.
6. To warn
   Watch out for the potholes.
7. To ask or request
   Put that in the corner, please.

Parts of a sentence

THE LANGUAGE KIT 2

Subject

The subject of a statement sentence:

- comes at or near the beginning of the sentence
- usually tells us what the sentence is about
- can be one word or a group of words.

If the subject is a single word it can be:

- a noun
- a pronoun.

Object

The object of a statement sentence:

- comes after the verb
- can be one word (a noun or a pronoun) or a group of words
- refers to a different person or thing from the subject.

Exception: words ending in '-self' or '-selves' in sentences like this: ***Eleanor cut herself on a piece of glass.***

The object is often something that is affected in some way by the verb. The objects in these sentences are underlined:

Pam has just eaten <u>my piece of cake</u>.
I wanted to eat <u>it</u>.

Verb

- A verb is an essential part of a sentence.
- In a statement sentence it normally comes after the subject.

We use verbs:

- to describe **actions**
  She <u>tumbled</u> over the edge.
- to describe **feelings and states of mind**
  I <u>love</u> sausage and chips for breakfast.

The verb in a sentence can be:

- **one word**
  She <u>ran</u> home.
- **a group of words**
  I <u>have been thinking</u> about that.

More about verbs

Past, present and future

We can write about the past, the present or the future. One way of showing this is by the **tense** of the verb.

The past

Writing about the past can include:

- history books
- diaries
- newspaper reports describing things that have happened
- autobiography (writing about your own life).

The future

Writing about the future can include:

- weather forecasts
- horoscopes
- newspaper reports describing things that are planned
- personal plans.

The present tense

There are two forms of present tense in English:

	Simple present	Present continuous
I	walk	am walking
she	walks	is walking

The **simple present** is used for:

- repeated actions
  She walks to school every day.
- things that are always true
  They live in Sunderland.
- some commentaries
  Zola shoots! – It's a goal!
- some stories
  So he says to me …

The **present continuous** is used for actions that are still going on. For example:

The Queen is talking to the crowd.

GRAMMAR REFERENCE

The past tense

The past tense has two different forms:

- the simple past
- the past continuous.

Forming the simple past tense

The **simple past** tense of **regular** verbs ends in *-d*:

I save → *I saved*
I walk → *I walked*
I cry → *I cried*
I play → *I played*
I tap → *I tapped*

Some verbs are **irregular**. That means that they do not follow this rule. For example:

I run → *I ran*
I go → *I went*
I hit → *I hit*

Forming the past continuous tense

We make the **past continuous** tense of all verbs like this:

I save → *I was saving*
I walk → *I was walking*
I cry → *I was crying*
I play → *I was playing*
I tap → *I was tapping*

We use *was* or *were* followed by the *-ing* form of the verb. All verbs follow this rule.

Using the simple past and the past continuous tenses

We use the past continuous if we want to tell people that the thing we are describing went on for some time:

She was walking slowly along the road.

We use the simple past to show that the thing we are describing is completed, or has ended:

I caught sight of Susan. She was walking slowly along the road.

Parts of the verb

Verbs have these parts:

Stem	*walk*	*go*
Present tense	*walk/walks*	*go/goes*
Past tense	*walked*	*went*
Present participle	*walking*	*going*
Infinitive	*to walk*	*to go*

Nouns

We use nouns to refer to:

- people
- ideas
- things
- mixtures of all three.

Most nouns will fit into one or more of the spaces in sentences like these:

That is a(n) _________ .
There are many _________ s.
_________ is very important.

These are all nouns:
mother rope happiness town Wayne

Common and proper nouns

Nouns can be divided into two groups:

- **Proper nouns** are the names of particular people, places, books, TV programmes, films and things like that. They are written with a capital letter at the beginning:
  John Smith
  London
  Starship Enterprise
- **Common nouns** are all the other nouns that are not proper nouns.

Pronouns

Pronouns refer back to something that has already been mentioned in a piece of writing. They can refer back to:

- a word – like a noun or another pronoun
- a group of words, a phrase
- an idea.

We use pronouns to avoid repeating things. It is important to make sure that the reader understands exactly what each pronoun refers to. There are several different types of pronoun, but some of the commonest are personal pronouns.

Personal pronouns

Personal pronouns are used instead of the names of people and things. They have two forms:

Subject	**Object and other uses**
I	*me*
we	*us*
she	*her*
he	*him*
they	*them*

The only ones that don't have two forms are:

you	*you*
it	*it*

We use the pronouns in the first column as the **subject** of the sentence and the ones in the second column the rest of the time:

I don't like dogs.
This dog came up to me.
Then it bit me.

Person and number

Pronouns can be **singular** or **plural**. They are also described as being **1st**, **2nd** or **3rd** person.

	Singular	**Plural**
1st person	*I/me*	*we/us*
2nd person	*you*	*you*
3rd person	*he/him*	
	they/them	
	she/her	
	it	

So 'I' is '1st person singular', 'we' is '1st person plural', and so on.

Possessives

There are two other forms of the personal pronoun 'I/me':

- **my** – the form we use with a noun, to show possession
  That's my book.
- **mine** – the form we use on its own to show possession.
  That book is mine.

This gives us this set:

I	*me*	*my*	*mine*
we	*us*	*our*	*ours*
you	*you*	*your*	*yours*
she	*her*	*her*	*hers*
he	*him*	*his*	*his*
it	*it*	*its*	*its*

Adjectives

Adjectives are sometimes called 'describing words'.
We can use them in two ways:

Adjectives with nouns
We use adjectives before nouns. They give more information about the noun:

a car
a new car
a new red car
a new shiny red car.

All the underlined words are adjectives.

Adjectives to tell us more about subjects
We also use adjectives in sentences after verbs like 'be'. They come after the verb and tell us more about the subject of the sentence:

My car (SUBJECT) *is* *red.* (ADJECTIVE)

Comparative and superlative

When we compare things we sometimes use a different form of the adjective:
high – higher – highest

Sometimes we use an extra word before the adjective:
interesting – more interesting – most interesting

We say that *higher* and *more interesting* are the **comparative** forms of *high* and *interesting* – we are comparing them. *Highest* and *most interesting* are the **superlative** forms.

Important

1. You can only **compare** *two* things or people.
2. You must have at least *three* to use the **superlative**: you can't have 'the best of two'.

-er/-est or more/most?

1. All one-syllable words add *-er/-est*.
2. Most words of more than one syllable use *more/most*.
3. Some two-syllable words add *-er/-est*:
   - words ending in *-y*
   - *clever* and *quiet*
4. A few three-syllable words add *-er/-est*:
   unhappy *unlucky*
5. A small group of words can add *-er/-est* or use *more/most*:
   common *cruel*
   gentle *narrow*
   pleasant *polite*
   shallow *simple*
   stupid

Phrases

A phrase is a group of words that work together as part of a sentence.

Noun phrases

A noun phrase can be the subject or the object of the sentence. It is built up on a noun or a pronoun. In these noun phrases the noun is underlined:

Subject (noun phrase)	Rest of sentence
Chips	*are revolting.*
Those chips	*are revolting.*
Those soggy chips	*are revolting.*
Those cold soggy chips	*are revolting.*

In these examples all the words have been added **before** the noun. You can also add them **after** it:

Those cold soggy chips on your plate ...

Adjective phrases

Instead of using a single adjective, like 'fast', you can add to its meaning by putting one or more words before it:

fast
very fast
fantastically fast
absolutely ultra mega fast.

These words (*very, fantastically*, etc.) **modify** (change) the meaning of the adjective. The group of words is called an **adjective phrase**. You can use an adjective phrase wherever you can use an adjective.

Modifying words

There are two groups of words that we can use in this way:

- words that **add to the strength of the adjective**, like *very, terribly, really*
- words that **reduce the strength of the adjective**, like *fairly, slightly, a bit*.

Verb phrases

The verb in a sentence can be a single word or a group of words, a phrase. In these sentences, the verb is underlined:

The car was travelling too fast.
It crashed.
They were saving up for a holiday.
They visited Italy last year.

If the sentence verb contains more than one word, you will often find that it includes words like these:

am/is/are	*was/were*
have/has	*had*
do/does	*did*
shall/will	*should/would*
can	*could*
may	*might*